The

SHIRLEY TEMPLE

Scrapbook

The SHIRLEY TEMPLE *Scrapbook*

Loraine Burdick

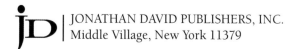
JONATHAN DAVID PUBLISHERS, INC.
Middle Village, New York 11379

Jonathan David Publishers, Inc.
68-22 Eliot Avenue
Middle Village, New York 11379

www.jdbooks.com

2 4 6 8 10 9 7 5 3 1

Library of Congress Cataloging-in-Publication Data

Burdick, Loraine
    The Shirley Temple scrapbook / Loraine Burdick.
        p. cm.
    Includes index.
    ISBN 0-8246-0449-0
        1. Temple, Shirley, 1928-   I. Title
PN2287.T33 B8 2001
791.43'028'092—dc21
[B]   2001028904

Book design and composition by John Reinhardt Book Design

Printed in China

*To everyone who
has ever loved Shirley*

ACKNOWLEDGMENTS

THANKS ARE DUE the many collectors of memorabilia and fans of Shirley Temple that I have met through the years, as well as some meticulous researchers. In particular, I would like to express my gratitude to Lucille McClure, Lillian Spencer, Lou Valentino, Pat Schoonmaker, JoAnn Janzen, Candice Corbridge, and Florence Gill. My thanks also go to the studios where Shirley Temple worked, especially Twentieth Century-Fox; the various movie magazines, mainly *Photoplay*, which regularly printed film cast lists in addition to their reviews; and members of the United States government, who had the wisdom to recognize Shirley's off-screen talents and give her the opportunity to use them.

A special note of thanks is due my son-in-law, Chuck (Mac Guy) Noll, who taught me how to use a computer so that I could prepare the manuscript efficiently.

Most of all, thanks to that Super-Extraordinary Ambassador Shirley Temple Black and her husband, Charles Alden Black.

CONTENTS

PREFACE

SHIRLEY TEMPLE has enjoyed comparing herself to that famous canine Rin-Tin-Tin as a star of enduring popularity. It would be equally appropriate, I would suggest, to compare her to Disneyland.

As a child, reading adventure books and fairy tales gave my imagination new roads to explore, new avenues to travel. Similarly, reading about Shirley Temple and saving photographs of her from newspapers and magazines in scrapbooks opened the door to a special "Shirleyland" in my life. And in time I met others who found a similar haven in this happy place where good people could forget hand-me-down clothes, personal clumsiness, and implacably straight hair. In Shirleyland we could tag along as she overcame obstacles through song, dance, charm, and kindness.

Some of us derived enormous pleasure from wearing Shirley outfits, collecting Shirley dolls, or by simply trying to look and act like Shirley. Many dreamed of someday having her fame or fortune. I, however, could enter the ecstasy of Shirleyland by merely wearing a hairbow or carrying a tablet with a Shirley Temple cover to first grade.

My older sister, Iris, saved Shirley photographs, and I got any she didn't want. I vividly recall her coming home one day and eagerly telling me that she had just seen Shirley in the movie *Heidi*. Her enthusiasm was contagious. Even experiencing the film secondhand gave me a glorious feeling. To hold on to that feeling, I collected everything from dolls to paper, ideas, dreams. When the Sunday newspaper carried front-page color photos of a gorgeous teenage Shirley in *Kathleen*, I was overjoyed. Luckily, by then Iris was grown up and I had first dibs on the pictures.

In adulthood, my Shirleyland collection continued to grow. With each newly acquired picture or item, I experienced a momentary return to childhood. As I continued to meet others whose fondness for Shirley was equal to mine, I discovered that each person, to my surprise, had his or her own special Shirleyland memories.

The Shirley Temple Scrapbook will take you on a journey to a wonderful part of your own past. It will enable you to recapture some of the joyous moments you experienced while watching Shirley's films, leafing through pictures you collected, or treasuring Shirley tie-ups and wearables. So, in a real sense, this book is for you, the fan. But it is also my hope that the *Scrapbook* will help others understand why we treasure Shirley as we do.

It is important to recognize that Shirley Temple outgrew her youth to become more than a child star. She has made outstanding contributions to the betterment of the world and its peoples. We must respectfully let her continue her service. The best way to thank Shirley Temple Black for the countless hours of pleasure she has given us is to appreciate her *whole* life, to look forward to further contributions, and to let her do what she chooses and does best—with our deepest and most heartfelt gratitude.

Loraine Burdick

Part One

A MAGICAL GIFT

BY THE TIME she was six years old, the Hollywood moguls referred to her as "Little Miss Miracle." Irvin S. Cobb, in presenting the young star a miniature Oscar in 1935, called her "the world's greatest gift of joy and happiness."

The extraordinary gift of which Mr. Cobb spoke was the beloved Shirley Jane Temple, born to parents Gertrude and George, in Santa Monica, California, on April 23, 1928. Shirley weighed a very average six and one-half pounds at birth, but with her arrival, the Temple world—which included big brothers John (Jack), age twelve, and George, Jr. (Sonny), age eight—now seemed complete.

Despite their joy, for the Temple family and others of that era shadows were gathering that suggested trouble ahead. Problems on farms had already spread to the cities, and the crash of 1929 left everyone uneasy or just plain terrified. The Temples faced the future with a tight budget, George's job at the bank, and one special splurge on the part of Gertrude: a coupon, purchased from a photographer, which guaranteed that a portrait of Shirley would be taken every six months until she was two years old, and after that once a year until her sixth birthday. The Temple boys being older, Gertrude had plenty of time to devote to her precious baby girl. There was plenty of sunshine despite the shadows.

Mother Gertrude once admitted, "Long before she was born, I tried to influence her future life by association with music, art, and natural beauty. Perhaps this prenatal preparation helped make Shirley what she is today." When Shirley was a toddler, Mrs. Temple did everything possible to guarantee her daughter a bright future. Parental supervision, regular exercise, and good eating were paramount. As a result, Shirley didn't contract the typical childhood illnesses—although she did end up suffering through them as an adult with her own children.

How the Magic Began

Like most women of the day, Gertrude Temple played the radio as she did her housework. She often sang along, and Shirley mimicked her mom, keeping time to the music. Mother and daughter particularly enjoyed their dance-and-skip steps—the kind of pure fun Mrs. Temple had not experienced

(Above left) Shirley at about two years—with more hair and an increasingly mature expression.

(Above right) Shirley, dressed in a bonnet, enjoyed the sunshine from the restraint of her playpen on the front lawn of the family's Santa Monica home.

(Below left) This photo of Shirley holding a basket is most likely the photographer's pose for the eighteen-months coupon. It is difficult to identify the photo precisely, because no dates were given. Further complicating matters is the fact that Shirley's age was twice "reduced" by Fox publicists in order to make her appear more precocious, the result being that many poses were incorrectly identified in studio biographies.

(Below right) By the age of three, the smile and flirty eyes were well established, but the curls were still coming along. This photo carries the signature of that photo coupon seller, G. Edwin Williams.

during her own rather conservative upbringing. Shirley displayed grace, a keen sense of rhythm, and a genuine delight in moving about to music. At lunchtime, Gertrude entertained Shirley with letter and number games. Many mothers of the day engaged in this home-schooling version of our modern Head Start program, and Shirley loved the interaction. She also demonstrated that she was a very capable child.

Fooling with Magic

By the the tender age of three, Shirley had already entered the public arena. It is difficult to unravel many details of Shirley's early life. As soon as she succeeded at Fox in 1934, the studio reported her a year younger than she actually was. When compiling a full studio biography a few months later, a false birth certificate was prepared and distributed, giving Shirley's birth year as 1929, not 1928. The hand-lettered date, the signatures, including even that of Shirley's obstetrician, Dr. Leo J. Madsen, all looked better than on the original, which was not published until after 1940. Details of babyhood development as recorded in mother Gertrude's baby book were edited and revised, all to support the 1929 birth date. Similarly, many other details of Shirley's childhood were changed.

Many people claimed credit for "discovering" Shirley, though accurate information now suggests that Gertrude Temple doggedly merchandised her daughter until others recognized her magical appeal. When Fox publicists took over, every word seemed to describe an angelic genius. Mrs. Temple worked to counteract some of this exaggeration with her own interviews, also restricting the access of those who strayed too far into hyperbole. Many interviewers were refused; others were required to submit copy to Mrs. Temple for approval. Most responsible for destroying the myth of perfection is Shirley's own autobiography, *Child Star*, published in 1988, which seems to point to mother Gertrude herself as the person responsible for the magic.

According to studio publicity, Shirley was three years of age in this photo. Actually, she is older, with her hair all specially curled for a performance.

Sound films were new in 1928, and they quickly demonstrated that music recorded better than dialogue. Dance numbers and singing became the big ticket, and countless studios sprang up to train would-be movie stars. Shirley's mom had definite ideas about giving her daughter professional dance training, but it is actually father George who indirectly determined which school she would attend. As it happened, a valued customer at the bank where George worked, one Ethel Meglin, heard the proud daddy brag about his offspring. Mrs. Meglin suggested that Shirley take classes at her own studio. And so, Shirley was enrolled in the Santa Monica branch of Meglin Dance Studios. Although biographies have repeatedly reported that Mrs. Temple thought it would be *fun* for Shirley to attend dancing school, one other aspect

surely was not overlooked: the studio would present all children in regular public recitals for parents and other interested parties. Shirley's magic would have a sponsor.

Shirley gave private demonstrations just for the family, and everyone found her "happy stepping" infectious. Gertrude was thankful that, although showered with attention, Shirley did not develop an outsized ego. Instead, she seemed to just enjoy sharing her happiness with others.

THE MEGLIN ENROLLMENT CARD, reproduced in the December issue of *Screen Guide* magazine, reveals that Shirley, student #203, began classes in the main studio on September 13, 1931. The adorable three-and-a-half-year-old with brown eyes and blonde hair lived at 948 24th Street, Santa Monica, California. Shirley "soon became [the] star pupil" at Meglin Dance Studios, Mrs. Temple was quoted as saying in the March 1935 issue of *Silver Screen* magazine. The June issue of *Modern Screen* described the dance class as consisting of "curtsying girls and solemn-bowing boys," while another writer described the first class as being filled with "wildly sliding boys" whom Shirley joined. By that Christmas, the Santa Monica newspaper reported a studio public performance.

Some four months after Shirley began dance lessons, excitement ran high at the studio. A talent scout, the parents had been advised, would soon be visiting Meglin to interview the students and cast some in a movie. When that important day arrived, it was obvious that the mothers—except for Mrs. Temple, that is—had dressed their children to perfection, hoping to impress the visitor. For some reason, Gertrude was unaware of the casting call, and Shirley arrived wearing her usual blue practice costume.

Upon seeing the well-attired crowd of children, and perhaps embarrassed that her tot was not dressed for the occasion, Mrs. Temple took Shirley in hand and began to head for the school exit. A teacher stopped them and urged Gertrude to let the scout see Shirley just as she was, and Shirley soon joined the other children in parading before the gentleman while the mothers waited anxiously outside. "As I look back, I think it was not ambition. It was just curiosity that made me do it,"

Mrs. Temple said in the February 1935 issue of *American Magazine*.

After auditioning all the children, the scout left Meglin quickly and without a word. The following week at lesson time, another movie scout appeared. This time, Shirley and another girl hid behind the piano, no doubt more a display of impishness than of shyness. The second scout, Charles Lamont, a director for Educational Studios, coaxed the two children out of hiding. Lamont was immediately captivated by Shirley, and he selected her for a part in an unnamed movie that Educational was about to make.

MANY DETAILS OF THESE first film studio arrangements are hard to sort out; much was obscured deliberately because of the desperation to somehow get money. It is certain that the concept of using little children to imitate or parody adult stars came from Jack Hays. Even this was surely an outgrowth of the mid-twenties art of C.H. Twelvetrees. The Twelvetrees kiddies appeared regularly in *Pictorial Review* and elsewhere acting like much older children involved in sports and society activities where top hats and upper garments were set off by droopy oversized diapers with large center safety pins. This was how Hays presented what became known as the "Baby Stars" in his Baby Burlesks.

Hays secured essential backing—some 75 percent of the budget—from Universal Studios. Charles Lamont came on board and was billed as the director of each short film; Jack Hays was billed as the producer. However, information from those present and even photographs taken on the set demonstrate the proprietary role of Hays, as did his later lawsuits against the Temples, in which he claimed responsibility for training Shirley.

Although Universal Studios met with the Temples, neither the studio nor Hays had a legal contract with Shirley. The proposed contract with Universal was for two years, some twenty-four films, and lots of fringe benefits, but actual money was paid only for days worked. With the Depression in full swing, every possible corner was cut or promise made just to make a little cash. Nobody wanted to detail any of this shady business until Al Hicks came along.

Al Hicks had the job, if only semiofficial, of recruiting talent for Jack Hays and his Educational Films, Educational Studios, and then Educational Studios, Inc. By the time Fox was controlling Shirley's publicity, Hicks spilled the sour grapes in an article entitled "Who Made Shirley Temple?," published in 1936 in *Rural Progress* magazine. The small publication had paid him for the piece, and because his details were so different from other respectable accounts, they were considered suspect. However, *Child Star* seems to corroborate much of what Hicks wrote.

In *Rural Progress*, Hicks depicted wild, uncontrolled children at the dance studio, whereas Shirley depicts the wild ranting and raving as taking place on the Educational lot. Hicks claimed, contrary to other information, that Mrs. Temple worked to get appearances for Shirley at local affairs before she was "discovered" at Meglin. Shirley writes of appearing at a benefit where Will Rogers was the master of ceremonies. One thing is certain: the article in *Rural Progress* gave the magazine a huge boost in popularity and gave Hicks a much-needed check. In addition, it contained a good deal of otherwise unknown facts.

Shirley Goes to Work

Before Christmas 1931, Shirley and the other children selected by Hays began work at Educational Studios, located in a rented space on what was called Poverty Row in Los Angeles. There was no pay, not even for expenses, until actual filming began. Away from parental eyes, the children were guided, rehearsed, trained, and bullied. Shirley wrote of a black box used as an isolation chamber to quiet down or cool off difficult children. To aid in the latter, she speaks of the chamber containing a block of ice.

The Educational movie was to be a parody of the major film *The Front Page*, with the derisive title *The Runt Page*. Where to stand, how to move, and where to look were drilled into the children by top sergeants Hays and Lamont. After about ten days of training, during which time Shirley was suffering from a cold brought on by that isolation box ice, it was announced that actual filming—and remuneration—would begin after the New Year.

Shirley's first day of filming turned out to be a superdud. The little star did not twinkle. Time was money, and if Shirley could not perform as leading lady, they would have to get the "other" little girl, Audrey Rae Leonard. Audrey was absolutely beautiful, but she lacked Shirley's sparkle, and Shirley had been prepared to spoof the all-powerful gossip columnist Louella Parsons. Audrey was told to be ready to take over the next day if necessary.

That evening, Shirley's cold led to a further complication—an abscessed ear. Her doctor lanced the ear, relieving the pain and pressure of inflammation, and the next morning he accompanied Shirley, her mother, and father to the studio to assure the powers-that-be that Shirley was able to work. This time, Shirley performed magically, which was quite remarkable since Shirley quotes her mother's record as saying that the day consisted of eleven-and-a-half hours with two naps. The first paycheck was for $10.00, and the family was excited and grateful. Things were tough everywhere, even at the bank, and this was more than many adults were earning in a week. The Temples hoped that many more opportunities awaited Shirley.

The Baby Burlesks

Educational Films Corporation, a subsidiary of Educational Pictures, Inc., was perhaps Jack Hays's fancy name for the distribution arm of his little empire. He generated the ideas, wrote the scripts, and most of the other work as well. During 1932, Hays made the one-reel Burlesks, with each short subject running about ten or eleven minutes. He also created fill-in films with other topics.

For Shirley, each of her films required about four days' shooting. Then there were assorted unpaid rehearsal days and publicity photo shoots. The publicity was both for films and for products such as Baby Ruth candy bars, which helped to fund the remaining 25 percent of the film costs. The first signed, although not legally notarized, contract with Hays's Universal Studios sponsor specified $50.00 a week as Shirley's salary, but this was for actual filming. It also detailed what she would get if Universal or Hays secured other employment in her behalf.

The original plan was that the Burlesks would

(continued on page 11)

When Jack Hays worked his Baby Stars, he supposedly began with play and friendly visiting. No mothers were allowed, as they often would give their children directions that conflicted with those of Hays. Also, they would have insisted that Hays curtail his discipline methods, as detailed in Shirley's autobiography.

Hays's efforts were successful, and soon he had the children and pups relaxed and happy.

The full staff of Jack Hays included the children—with star Shirley center front, on the producer's lap, and Danny Boone to her left. With them is "a complete staff of teachers, coaches, as well as nurses, who carefully watch over the well-being of each child," as quoted from the caption of this mid-1932 King Features release. The photo, whether a temporary situation or totally staged, presented Educational Studios as very nurturing to its children, which would certainly make people more receptive to the films.

Mrs. Temple redesigned Shirley's Baby Burlesk diaper so that it was actually a panty. When one views the films, it is easy to see that Shirley's clothes fit snugly while those of others have a definite and deliberate sag. However, in appearance, this also identifies Shirley as "the star." Mrs. Temple made blouses to fit Shirley's characters, styled her hair, and served in every possible way to keep Shirley ready to shine. However, she did not coach Shirley or guide her lines; that was all done by Hays.

Part of the funding for the Baby Burlesks came from advertising. Ice cream and other treats were served to keep the stars happy or to reward them. Shirley poses here with her Sunfreeze Ice Cream cup.

Here, the children enjoy assorted ice cream treats—without mothers rushing in to protest spills on the obviously good clothes. Not in the photo are the children who played maids, cannibals, aides, and Indians.

have adult voices dubbed to sound cutesy—simperingly childish—but the lines had to be filmed as spoken by the children in order to synchronize the mouthing of each word. It was discovered that the childish voices had much comic charm, so only sound effects and music were added as occasional enhancements.

The second Burlesk, *War Babies*, was a takeoff on the World War I film *What Price Glory?* Shirley imitated Dolores Del Rio, playing a little French coquette. Her first quoted screen dialogue was from this film: "*Mais oui, mon cher.*" Shirley had her own little soldier boys to flirt with and vamp seductively, and she overcame competition from the other girls with a toss of her bare shoulder or a kiss.

DURING 1932, SHIRLEY acted with Georgie Smith, Danny Boone, and others in a total of seven one-reeler Baby Burlesks for Educational. She impersonated Louella Parsons as Lulu Parsnips and Marlene Dietrich as Morelegs Sweetrick. Georgie was Raymond Bunion of newspaper fame and then Frightwig von Stumblebum, a Von Stroheim takeoff in top hat, complete with three Yes Men. To Danny's Tarzan, Shirley played a missionary called Diaperzan.

By contrast, each year the Western Association of Motion Picture Advertisers, better known by the acronym Wampas, selected a group of young ladies in their late teens or early twenties and gave them the name "Baby Stars." Perhaps so called because they were grooming themselves to become movie stars, the photogenic young ladies were selected to promote the film industry and individual photographers. Some of the girls actually appeared in films, giving legitimacy to the

(Above) For the special 1933 Wampas presentation, there were quite a few photos of Shirley in her long gown. She took it very seriously.

(Left) One Wampas grouping was a wedding fashion show staged for a Hollywood Assistance League charity benefit. Here, Shirley as flower girl happily leads bride Gloria Stuart and her attendant, Anita Louise. Notice that the billing reads "Shirley Jane Temple" rather than just "Shirley Temple," as she was credited in Educational Studios' short subjects. This became an actual cover for a brochure distributed to soon-to-be brides, with space for engagement and wedding details and memories.

promotion. Others were talented hopefuls, even if their only talent was beauty. Wampas Baby Stars made special appearances, participated in benefits, and posed for freelance as well as studio photographers—anything that might lead to newspaper and magazine coverage and ultimately stimulate movie attendance.

The yearly Wampas selection had been going on since 1930, but never with a child, let alone an actual baby. Then, for 1933 (but presented early), there was a sudden change in the promotion. Shirley had received some nice publicity, both in connection with her films at Educational Studios and because she was such an adorable, photogenic tot. She became a Wampas selection, joining Lona Andre, Anita Louise, Eleanor Holm, Gloria Stuart, and Ginger Rogers, among others. All were hopeful that having been chosen as Wampas girls would give their careers a boost.

Photographers came with ideas for poses. Studio publicists came with ways to steer advertising. Everyone worked, as others did each year, so that the Wampas presentation would bring in big dividends of cash. This was all rather like a coming-out party for movie debutantes, with the end purpose being a lucrative career rather than a successful "society" marriage.

The Frolics Begin

The performers in the kiddie capers had long since outgrown their diapers. Shirley was old enough to deliver longer scenes with dialogue and actions. At this time, the issue of censorship had emerged as an important one, for Hollywood films were being criticized for containing immoral or risqué situations. Even the Baby Burlesks, which occasionally used double-entendres, were sometimes characterized as crude.

While one last Burlesk was made without Shirley, she did several small bits in feature films. Meanwhile, Hays determined that a new venue could be pursued. These were the Frolics of Youth, two-reel films running about twenty-two minutes, each telling a full story. In the Frolics, Shirley was part of the Rogers family and each film revolved around a different family adventure. As little sister, Shirley was in turn impish, annoying, and troublesome, but still loving. As before, she played to both characters and audience with magical appeal. The realistic stories were centered around struggle and loyalty, making for wholesome and happy films.

The Frolics contained some very realistic action. Shirley fought with her screen brother (Junior Coughlin), and a line was set up dividing her side of the room from his. Her constant annoying of Junior was set aside in the interest of love and family loyalty when he got into a fight with a supersnob rich boy played by Kenneth Howell. Shirley stabbed Ken in the backside with a fork and gave the utensil an astonishing bend. Oh, those props!

For Baby Burlesks' and Frolics' publicity, Shirley wore her own clothes. She grew slowly, so she was able to wear outfits over a period of two or three years, always looking just right. The pleated pink dress with lace collar worn for Burlesk publicity was worn in the 1932 Frolic *Dora's Dunking Doughnuts* and in the 1933 feature film *The Red-Haired Alibi*. It was also used for assorted publicity. The blue cloth polo coat from 1933's *Managed Money* was also worn for publicity purposes.

During her time at Educational, Shirley began fashion tie-ups, thereby influencing girls' styles. In 1932, *Photoplay* included a Shirley photo and instructions for creating a Shirley Temple coiffure as part of its regular fashion hints, which up to this time were aimed at adults. Women's magazines began to analyze her dress style, recommending the flattering line of a dress as hanging gracefully from the shoulder or a high yoke.

Rosenau Brothers, of New York, secured a license to produce dresses carrying the Shirley Temple name and endorsement, and began their hugely successful Cinderella line. The first Cinderella line was the Hollywood 2-in-1 Dress, which was offered in at least four different styles. (Only four photos of the designs have turned up so far.) They were actually a sunsuit with matching sundress to be worn together or separately.

Whether Shirley outgrew these styles or Cinderella decided to create new Shirley designs, by 1935 the "Hollywood 2-in-1" Dress sets had been renamed Twosomes; they were then promoted by Carol Ann Beery, adopted daughter of

(continued on page 16)

Shirley wore this dress in the Frolic *Merrily Yours. Here she is signing for Fox's casting director, Phil Friedman. This was publicity for* Fox Follies, *which became* Stand Up and Cheer.

The blue coat with matching beret, as shown here, was worn in Managed Money. *This still is by photographer Otto Dyar for Fox Film publicity.*

(Opposite) Once again, here is the Managed Money *coat and beret outfit, now a publicity pose for* Fox Follies. *It was suggested as a fashion idea, with the tiny collar worn up or down. However, in much of the United States a coat this short would have been considered in need of lengthening or suitable as a hand-me-down for a smaller child.*

actor Wallace Beery. The designs were the same. The American Character 1935 dolls of Carol Ann were dressed in the Twosome outfits. Meanwhile, Ideal Novelty & Toy Co., Inc., had created Shirley Temple dolls, and these were outfitted in copies of Shirley's own wardrobe and film dresses.

WHILE MRS. TEMPLE worked to line up acting opportunities for her daughter, continually hoping that a good role in a big film would finally establish Shirley as a star, big brothers Jack and Sonny went on with their lives, finding that little sister's filming and publicity obligations interfered with their right to be individuals or just ordinary big brothers. Nonetheless, they didn't seem to harbor jealousy or resentment. Mr. Temple concluded that Shirley's earnings were not sufficient to enable the family to recoup its investment and suggested that the dream be abandoned. But Mrs. Temple proceeded to exploit every possible contact.

Jack Hays, like many other go-getters, played a few angles of his own. He secured some work for

Here is a "Hollywood 2-in-1" outfit designed by Cinderella. Shirley stands on a camera dolly at Educational Studios, while the photo advertising identifies her as the Famous Child Star of the Frolics of Youth comedies.

Each "Hollywood 2-in-1" outfit had a matching sunsuit that could be worn underneath or separately. The significance of the pie and doghouse is unknown.

Shirley by contacting friends, and in each case got most of her earnings as per the original contract. An acquaintance, Gene Mann, agreed to find work for Shirley, but evidently only scored big after she was a success. His contact for a personal appearance in New York was rejected, so he sued.

The Temples felt that they could handle everything: Mrs. Temple would accompany Shirley and meet her needs; Mr. Temple would keep track of money and business, as would befit the man of the family. He had no experience with contracts or business law, but when Jack Hays filed for bankruptcy on October 25, 1933 (Shirley says September 28), Mr. Temple did note one special item: Shirley's contract was not listed as part of Hays's assets. Father George bought up the contract through court overseers for $25.00 and later was successful in defending against lawsuits in which Hays claimed a cut of all of Shirley's by then sizable earnings on the basis of original agreements and the training he provided.

As Shirley became increasingly known, opportunists were eager to capitalize on her popularity. Fans were able to find George at the bank, and some opened accounts there, which in turn gave him increased importance and a higher salary. But so many people came along proposing schemes or wanting favors that many problems arose. It was clear that Shirley's career now needed the full-time attention of both parents.

IT IS DIFFICULT to trace Shirley's early acting career with precision. There were, of course, the opportunities that came from Educational's operations, but Mrs. Temple also visited many casting offices on her own, hunting for bit parts. She went through much anguish—and a great deal of shoe leather—trying to find just the right roles in which her little doll would sparkle. Her efforts brought Shirley assorted bits in some big movies but, alas, many of the roles were cut down to almost nothing by the time the film reached the screen. As with many supporting players, Shirley sometimes didn't get any billing.

Magic Needs an Audience

Actors hired by a studio to play bit parts were given instructions as to when to report and how to dress; then they sat and waited till needed. So Shirley would be brought in, wait to do what she was told, then stop off at payroll to pick up her check. Sometimes she made it to the screen, sometimes not. At times, her name appeared in the credits even though her role was merely a prop for adult action.

Shirley's first role at Paramount was one such part in the western *To the Last Man*, with Randolph Scott, with whom she would later star several times. She almost dismisses it in her autobiography, but it was a good bit, complete with location shooting and a quick paycheck.

Harpo Marx was making *Duck Soup* at Paramount at the time and, after seeing Shirley perform, he offered Mrs. Temple $50,000 to *adopt* Shirley. Incredible as it may seem, magazines reacted by writing about how nice it was that Shirley was valued so highly, none characterizing the offer as offensive, let alone illegal. Harpo may have seen potential value, but Paramount did not.

Paramount let Shirley go after the western, and Fox Film Corporation didn't keep her after she did a bit part in *Carolina*, which starred Janet Gaynor, Lionel Barrymore, and Robert Young. There were no contracts, no further promises—just a day or so of work. But somebody finally did recognize Shirley Temple's considerable potential. Was it at the preview of a Burlesk or a Frolic? Was it afternoon or evening? Reports are conflicting.

Accounts as to just how Shirley came to Fox for the role in *Stand Up and Cheer* vary with who was claiming to have "discovered" her. One account has it that there was a film showing at a local theater and Shirley was there to see herself on screen. That Fox songwriter Jay Gorney was also there indicates that someone was checking her out as a possibility for what at the time was a small song-and-dance number in a production very similar to a stage musical revue. In fact, the film's title was then *Fox Follies*, following a string of such films Fox began in 1929 when sound films were new. The first was *Fox Movietone Follies of 1929*.

Shirley gave Harpo Marx a playful sock to the jaw when she visited him at the Paramount commissary during the shooting of Duck Soup *in 1933. She was filming* To the Last Man *and again wore her pink pleated dress for publicity, though not in the movie.*

Houck began to smile: his search had ended. Jay Gorney and Gertrude Temple were ecstatic. Gorney had found a new talent—perhaps even a star—someone who might be able to "make" his songs, and Mrs. Temple had found someone who appreciated how precious her child truly was. *Fox Follies* would be Shirley Temple's first featured appearance in a film.

Aware that Shirley did in fact sparkle, Fox changed the name of *Fox Follies* to *Stand Up and Cheer*. The film remained a series of follies production numbers, some extravagant and some rather tawdry, with a flimsy storyline added to loosely connect the various acts. Then, suddenly, there was Shirley. In spite of heavy lipstick to match the scantily-clad chorus girls, Shirley emerged in her bouncy curls and full petticoats, and the nation's heart went right to her. Warner Baxter was the film's big star, but James Dunn, playing opposite Shirley, went to the top as Shirley's leading man. Audiences and critics did just as the film title suggested: they stood up and cheered—for Shirley Temple.

PEOPLE HAD COMPLAINED so much about immorality in movies that the United States Congress designated one of its own, by the name of Will Hays (no relation to Jack), to establish an official Board of Censors to "clean up the movies." It paid special attention to language, lack of costuming, including an emphasis on lingerie poses, and even the length of movie kisses. Will Hays meant to satisfy public consensus and clean up the movies. In serious financial trouble, Fox

After the showing, Mrs. Temple and Shirley waited near the box office while Mr. Temple went to bring the car around. Leo Houck, assistant director for Fox Film Corporation, and Jay Gorney approached the pair and struck up a casual conversation. They inquired as to whether Shirley could sing, and when told that she could, made an appointment for her to come to the studio the next day. Fox had been interviewing children for their upcoming musical, and having not yet found anyone suitable for the little girl part, pressures were mounting.

Shirley auditioned for Lew Brown, associate producer of *Fox Follies*. As a piano accompanist played "St. Louis Blues," Shirley did a buck-and-wing. Then she sang a song she'd heard Rudy Vallee sing on the radio a few days earlier. Mr.

Shirley appeared in a benefit for the Hollywood Assistance League once more. Again she wore the pink pleated dress, either because it was the best she owned or the most becoming. Dickie Moore joined Shirley to examine the Mickey and Minnie Mouse puppets from the show. Then they gave the puppets a tea party. A newspaper file date stamped on the photo back is "August 31, 1933, A.M.," with the comment that they played to capacity audiences. (The plural indicates that there were multiple showings.)

needed to clean up at the box office. Shirley gave both camps success. When she auditioned for Fox, she said, associate producer Lew Brown offered a two-year contract at $150 a week. So pleased was Fox with Shirley's work that Winfield Sheehan extended the contract to seven years.

When news of record New York attendance at *Stand Up and Cheer* reached Hollywood, Fox moved Shirley's name to a prominent position on the marquee. Immediate plans began for another Shirley Temple film.

Mrs. Temple was accused by some of seeking fame and fortune at her child's expense. Quite the contrary. Although excited, proud, and tearful over Shirley's having won the part in *Fox Follies*, Gertrude did not forsake her strict good sense about Shirley. More than likely, Gertrude was just a proud mother eager to share her very sweet child with others. Years later, she would explain her inner feelings as she saw so many people reach out and admire her daughter. But then, in 1934, the world was facing war overseas and financial depression in the United States. Shirley offered a comforting spot of joy and delight, and her mother rejoiced.

(continued on page 23)

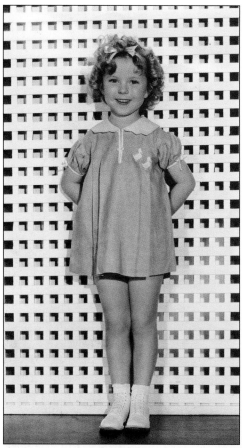

(Left top and bottom) Fox also prepared a series of fashion poses featuring Shirley, the purpose of which were to provide fashion suggestions. (Neither patterns nor actual clothes were for sale.) The children's styles included this light blue linen dress piped in white with scalloped collar. The back pose shows very tousled hair, delightfully natural.

(Below) The studio captioned this photo "Papa guards her pay check." George Temple was at the New Accounts window of their Santa Monica bank. However, a close look shows that this is a blank withdrawal check, not a salary deposit.

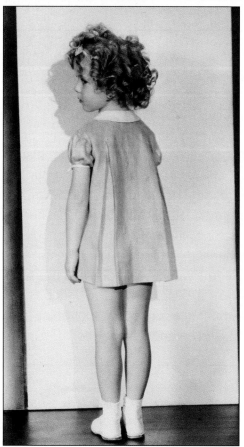

The Meglin school was considered opportunistic, pushy, and apt to claim tie-ups with Shirley, so Fox wanted to bury Shirley's Meglin connection. This 1934 photo was taken at the Elisa Ryan School of Dancing, which was considered more professional, more classy, and also probably more appreciative of Fox. Shirley is the star pupil in perfect costume; everyone else looks scruffy, but all bear the school's emblem.

Aware of Shirley's appeal, and on the verge of bankruptcy, Fox began to issue countless publicity poses of Shirley in her Stand Up and Cheer dotted dress. It worked. Each photo was just as adorable as this.

Announcing
The SHIRLEY TEMPLE

DOLL by IDEAL

● THE ONLY AUTHENTIC DOLL TO BE PRO-
DUCED UNDER THE "SHIRLEY TEMPLE" NAME.

● This newest Ideal doll will be an exact
replica of "Shirley Temple," the sweetheart
of America. She will come in an authentic
Shirley Temple dress, packed in an unusually
attractive Shirley Temple box and with a
Shirley Temple button.

« « Ideal Novelty & Toy Co. has received exclusive rights to
manufacture and sell Shirley Temple dolls with the consent of
the Fox Films Corp. It is a violation of the law to manufacture, sell, or handle unauthorized Shirley Temple dolls. » »

IDEAL NOVELTY & TOY CO.
273 Van Sinderen Ave., Brooklyn, N. Y.   Showrooms: 200 Fifth Ave., New York

When writing to Ideal Novelty & Toy Co., will you please mention PLAYTHINGS?

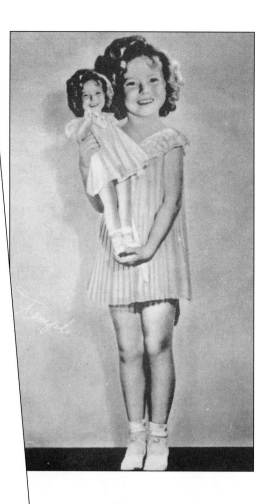

In the October 1934 Playthings, *Ideal announced the doll to
the toy trade. The usual schedule was to present Christmas
season toys at the April Toy Fair. The ad emphasized Ideal's
exclusive rights to the doll and essentially asked dealers to
order on trust and on anticipated Shirley publicity. Ideal ended
up shipping dolls by air express to fill the flood of orders.*

*Mrs. Temple hadn't yet approved Ideal's Shirley doll face, so
initial doll publicity used a Shirley photo as the doll's head.*

The Magic of Stardom

So began Shirley's meteoric rise: an actress at the age of four, a star at six, an Oscar-winner and number one box-office draw in the country from 1935 to 1938. She seemed like a live doll on the screen, so the Ideal Toy and Novelty Company—which had some experience with various tie-up dolls and was another firm badly in need of financial help—secured the licensing rights to create a doll in Shirley's likeness. Between the release of *Stand Up and Cheer* in May of 1934 and Ideal's first ad in *Playthings* that October, a great deal of work was done to get the doll ready for the big money to be made at Christmastime. The ad stated that the doll "will be an exact replica," and, in fact, first-published photos showed the doll and Shirley dressed alike and Shirley's photo head on the doll . . . a perfect likeness.

PARAMOUNT EXECUTIVES were beginning to pay attention to glowing reports from those who had been involved with Shirley in *To the Last Man*. Perhaps it was Harpo Marx or costar Randolph Scott who praised her so highly. No doubt, the box-office success of *Stand Up and Cheer* had caught Paramount's attention. They had tested and rejected Shirley for *Little Miss Marker* when she was a noncontract bit player. With Fox's added dramatic scenes between Shirley and James Dunn, it was obvious that she was more than a song-and-dance kid. The Damon Runyon story had been bought by Paramount two years earlier, but now Shirley was under contract to Fox, and Paramount would have to arrange—and pay much more—to have her loaned out. The deal was slow in being finalized but, having received the approval of Shirley's parents, Paramount began rehearsals and wardrobe fittings for Shirley.

Paramount released *Little Miss Marker* in June 1934. Following so close on the heels of her successful appearance in *Stand Up and Cheer*, *Marker* demonstrated Shirley's true star potential. Someone tried to persuade Mr. Temple to take Shirley to another studio for more money, as befitted her Paramount loan price. Instead, he went back to Fox with a request—$2,500 a week. Fox countered with an offer of $1,000. However, in late July 1934 a new Fox contract, negotiated by Winfield Sheehan, was signed. Fox had increased its offer to $1,250 a week, with increases built in over the next seven years, a substantial sum for the time. Some newspapers had encouraged Shirley to strike if Mr. Temple's request for a salary increase was denied. That would not be necessary, for the third contract soon gave Shirley $1,500 a week. By the

> Ideal Toy and Novelty did not create the first Shirley Temple doll. What seems to be the last pressbook of Educational Studios' short subjects distributed to theater owners announced dolls "modeled from a number of our Baby Stars, and which will be distributed in large quantities throughout the country. A doll of the beautiful Shirley Temple is now ready and several others will follow." The manufacturer was the Los Angeles Doll Company and the date was early 1934. Despite the quantity declared available, the marketing may have been limited, if there was any real marketing campaign at all. Or the dolls in question may just have been some of the interesting Japanese bisque style quickly adapted for sales promotion. Huge quantities of such dolls from Japan were on the market at the time.

time she made *Poor Little Rich Girl* in 1936, Shirley was earning $46,000 a picture.

The third Fox contract was unique in Hollywood for several reasons. The new Hays Office, charged with overseeing filmland decency, required that other star contracts contain a morality clause. No one even dared suggest that Shirley's agreements needed such a clause. Instead, her contracts specified that she receive no praise from coworkers, leaving that to her mother and directors and thereby protecting the child from smothering accolades. Shirley's contracts also specified that she was not to attend films of other actors lest she be tempted to copy their mannerisms. (Of

(continued on page 26)

(Above) This photo shows some Ideal doll costumes and others specially made up to copy Shirley's own clothes. The little coat has mittens attached to a ribbon through the sleeves to prevent loss. Shirley's dress is so short that it shows the matching panties, but ten years earlier these would have hung much lower and been called a romper suit.

(Right) Paramount immediately began publicity for Little Miss Marker, *including arranging for its star, Baby LeRoy, to take Shirley on a "date." Here they are returning home, and Shirley claimed a turn at the wheel. What a great car!*

(Opposite) Fox Film Corporation's assets were summed up in Will Rogers and Shirley Temple. In her autobiography, Shirley speaks of Will as the "lead horse in the studio's stable of stars." This setting is indeed a stable, and Will was busy making David Harum.

Mother Gertrude was almost always on the set so that, despite long waits, Shirley would be ready when needed. Here, the happy sharing is a book to read. Shirley is in costume; Gertrude is in her usual coat and hat.

No American company would assume the liability of insuring Shirley against accidents. A British firm covered her with a $25,000 policy that forbade her from flying in an airplane. (Soon, in *Bright Eyes*, Shirley sat in a plane as it taxied down a runway. However, the in-air scenes were done with rear-screen projection.) Shirley also was forbidden to go to war. The policy was important to Fox, since Shirley and Will Rogers were its Fort Knox both for earnings and for the 1935 merger with Twentieth Century. Had Will Rogers carried a similar policy, he wouldn't have died in a plane crash near Barrow, Alaska, the following August, leaving Shirley as the studio's sole major income-producer.

course, this was rescinded when Shirley had to mimic stars like Al Jolson, Eddie Cantor, Ginger Rogers, and Fred Astaire for a *Stowaway* performance.)

Mrs. Temple received a salary of $150 a week for the care and coaching of her daughter, and later also for being her sole hairdresser. By acting as the latter, Gertrude helped the studio substantiate publicity claims that Shirley's curls and hair color were natural. However, in reminiscing about losing out on the Dorothy role in *The Wizard of Oz*, Shirley commented that her father read the Oz books to her in the evenings while her mother fixed her hair with pins and curlers. To really pop the publicity balloon, Shirley added that her mother also used a cotton swab to dab on peroxide wherever some lightening was needed.

In a column dated April 19, 1938, Sheilah Graham wrote of being upset because she wanted to go to a fancy party. She called her favorite hairdresser, Ann Meredith, but Ann was "booked all day for Shirley Temple." Of course, such reports undermined studio claims that Shirley's hair color and curls were natural.

Publicity also insisted that no makeup was ever used on Shirley until *The Little Princess*, which was filmed in Technicolor. But photographs advertising curlers that would give girls Shirleylike curls showed her wearing heavy lipstick, and other color photos showed her with rouge and eyeliner. As early as *Little Miss Marker*, a photo showed Shirley at the makeup mirror powdering her nose. Shirley's autobiography details how all the "naturalness" was maintained after the earliest childhood honey-blonde hair began to darken steadily.

MRS. TEMPLE was essential to her daughter's success, and while her involvement helped foster a close mother-daughter relationship, it also meant that nearly all of Gertrude's time was devoted to Shirley. This called for many sacrifices on the part of the family. Although Gertrude hired a housekeeper and engaged a cook, each day was planned with Shirley's schedule in mind. There were the interviews, photo shoots, and costume fittings. There were also the sessions for which Shirley donned licensed "Shirley Temple" garments. An item could be considered a genuine Shirley article, said Mrs. Temple, only if it had been worn by her daughter, even for a few minutes. That policy notwithstanding, there are a fair number of photos in which Shirley is seen "wearing" a Cinderella dress that has obviously been superimposed on the dress she actually posed in, a post-production matter over which Mrs. Temple had no control. It also appears that in a series of dress shots the garment was slit in back so that it would slide on without touching Shirley's curls.

Mrs. Temple exercised considerable control over how many and which of the countless public figures of varying degrees of fame would be permitted to greet her daughter and pose for photos. She also was responsible for making sure that Shirley learned her lines for the next day's filming. The preparation required several evening read-throughs. This was followed by Shirley's rapid repetition of lines until she had them word-perfect. Mrs. Temple then slowed down Shirley's delivery, asking her to recite each phrase with proper speed, gesture, and emphasis. Although some fan magazines reported that all line readings were left to Shirley's discretion, this was in fact not the case.

The evening's rehearsal was followed by hair setting and grooming, a half-hour of play, and then bedtime. In the morning, Shirley still knew her lines perfectly, and often those of the other players as well. A viewing of Shirley's films suggests that her songs were similarly rehearsed, with expressions memorized. When a song is reprised,

(Top) Shirley was of school age by the fall of 1934, despite Fox's having reduced her stated age by a year. Here she is getting a reading lesson from her teacher, Mrs. W. M. Geddes. Concentrating in such busy surroundings was not easy.

(Bottom) Between school sessions, Shirley liked to "study" the filmmaking equipment. Here she looks through the camera finder. No one seems concerned about the welfare of the equipment.

On the Now and Forever *set, Shirley is entertained by Carole Lombard at a fancy piano. A grand piano was used in the film.*

the second delivery is nearly identical to the first. Still, some fan magazine features insisted that once Shirley and her mom returned home from a day's work, studio matters were not discussed.

WITH THE COMPLETION of *Little Miss Marker*, Shirley returned to Fox for *Now I'll Tell*, with Spencer Tracy, and especially for *Baby, Take a Bow*, in which she was able to capitalize on her song-and-dance success from *Stand Up and Cheer*. Then it was back to Paramount for *Now and Forever*. Mrs. Temple certainly earned her pay just keeping track of Shirley's ever-changing schedule.

During the shooting of *Now and Forever*, amateur cartoonist Gary Cooper taught Shirley to draw. He bought her a stuffed bear named Grumpy, identical to the Grumpy bear in the film. Whether this was child indulgence or intended to spare wear on the movie prop is uncertain. "To see a half-dozen celebrities on their knees, playing games with Shirley," wrote a reporter, "would give even the screen's most rabid denouncers new faith in its people and its future. Things *are* looking up for the reformers." Of course, it may well have been that Shirley was actually entertaining the adults!

Bright Eyes faced something of a rush to be ready for the big 1934 Christmas season. It was exciting for Shirley to visit the Glendale airport for location shooting, but crowds mobbed the airport fence and reached out to grab at her when she left. It was suddenly very obvious that the young star needed protection. So taken was the public with Shirley that some fans would visit the Temples' Santa Monica home, knock on the door, and ask to see their heroine. More brazen types would peer into the windows, hoping to get a glimpse of home and family.

Shirley and most of her costars became good friends. During the making of *Now and Forever*, Dorothy Dell, a previous friend from *Little Miss Marker* days, was killed in an automobile accident. Mournful cast members discussed the tragic loss of a young lady with such tremendous potential. When Shirley overheard the conversation, she burst into tears, only to be comforted by Carole Lombard. At that time, Shirley was scheduled to film a scene in which she would be sobbing after discovering that film daddy Gary Cooper was a thief. The result was a tremendously moving scene. Shirley later recalled the episode, wondering whether the timing had been deliberately staged so that her on-screen performance would be so convincing.

(continued on page 36)

McCALL'S, December, 1934.

McCALL'S, December, 1934.

Shirley Temple in "Now And Forever"

WEARS CHARMING LITTLE FROCKS
AND A SMART WINTER COAT

Miss Shirley and her dog, a prize dachshund. He is famous, too.

Shirley Temple, Fox Film star, world famous at the age of five.

Shirley in a scene with Carole Lombard in their new motion picture, "Now and Forever."

"Honor Bright?" asks Miss Shirley of Gary Cooper, in this scene.

8083

8075

No. 8075. Polka dotted silk dress with a white organdy collar bound with bias tape and pleated into the neckline to make it very perky. There are cunning matching panties under this dress.

No. 8083. Smart little coat with a double collar and turned back cuffs. Buttoned from neck to hem. The berét comes with it. The original is made of wool with a velvet collar and a velvet berét.

8083   8075

8084 8085

8085

8084

No. 8084. Crêpe de Chine party dress for white, pale pink or pale blue with white lace. This bertha collar, too, is pleated in at the neck—smarter than the gathered ones. There are panties to match underneath.

No. 8085. Challis dress with panties, and a charming white collar of linen. Pleated in the back to match the front. There are short very puffed up sleeves if you prefer them which make a party dress of it.

Shirley's movie fashions became such a hit that in the December 1934 issue of McCall's *magazine Shirley was featured wearing patterns adapted from her* Now and Forever *wardrobe. Now every mother could dress her darling like Shirley.*

Location shots for Now *and* Forever *were done at Lake Arrowhead, California. Shirley's lunch was called "hot soup" in the International News Bureau photo caption, but it became milk to promote the drinking of milk by children.*

Shirley visits the airport, where all the props are real, but she finds the sunlight very different from studio lighting and shields her eyes.

This pose of Shirley was included in the boxes with Ideal dolls. For Bright Eyes, it was also distributed at theaters with special advertising on the back. Theaters bought these—with backs blank to insert their theater's imprint and offer prizes—at $6.50 per thousand.

This ad promoting the General Electric kitchen used in the film backed the photo above. In Child Star, Shirley protested this unauthorized "licensing" by Fox.

Watch for this General Electric Kitchen in the new Shirley Temple hit **"Bright Eyes"** with Jimmy Dunn, starting Saturday, January 26th, at

El Portal Theatre

E. J. Sadler Company

GENERAL ELECTRIC APPLIANCES

5274 Lankershim Blvd., North Hollywood, Calif.

Telephone: North Holly. 50

ADDITIONAL COPIES OF PICTURE FREE TO ADULTS AT OUR STORE

(Left) Bright Eyes *contained some special Christmas scenes, but Shirley posed for others that would be distributed to the public. Everything was fake except for Shirley, her snowsuit, and the greeting to be displayed by the theater or passed out by the management to its patrons.*

(Opposite) During Bright Eyes, *Shirley posed in a police uniform to emphasize the importance of obeying traffic regulations. The National Safety Council hoped that the star would help influence both adults and children.*

(Right) Shirley shows the General Electric refrigerator used in Bright Eyes. *A series of these stills was offered for theater tie-up. They were placed in the windows of stores carrying the appliances, but the film's pressbook clearly states that publication in newspapers was strictly forbidden. This most likely meant that the licensing was controlled by the film studio, not by G.E.*

Enter VASSAR WAVER Contest
Win A Shirley Temple Doll.

MADE IN U.S.A.

TO MY FRIEND.......SHIRLEY TEMPLE

This color portrait, first introduced for Bright Eyes, *was supposedly autographed by Shirley. It announced the Vassar Waver, rubber curlers that would purportedly give any little girl Shirleylike curls.*

This Little Girl WON
A Shirley Temple Doll

Join the VASSAR WAVER CONTEST

Here is another winner of a Shirley Temple Doll

BEFORE and AFTER using VASSAR WAVER

For Croquignole or Shirley Temple headdress, start VASSAR WAVER at end of hair. Put the end through the slit in VASSAR WAVER, or if you wish, start it with your finger, as shown.

The wave is in the curl. Take each VASSAR WAVER down separately and comb the curl out flat and then comb them all together and finger your wave.

For :—

Spiral wave or wrap-around wave, you can twist the hair or roll it flat. You can make it crimpy by putting small amount of hair on VASSAR WAVER and you can make a flatter marcel by putting more hair on the curler.

Nine Shirley Temple dolls given to nine little girls every month.

Prizes To All Contestants

Dress Your Hair Like Shirley Temple and Send Your Picture in.

Directions

A large secret of success with VASSAR WAVERS is to roll your hair in the same direction every day and put the hair on VASSAR WAVER in the same place each day in order to deepen your curls and waves.

Do not use too much water if your hair is dry. Leave VASSAR WAVER in hair until thoroughly dry.

For long bob use spiral twist or make croquignole by starting VASSAR WAVER on the hair three inches from the scalp. Apply additional VASSAR WAVER to the ends.

For Oily Hair—Wash your hair with Caley Cream Shampoo before applying VASSAR WAVER.

For Dry Hair—Wash with VASSAR Treatment.

W. J. CALEY and CO., INC.
Philadelphia, Pa.

Promotion of the Vassar Waver demonstrated its effectiveness in curling little girls' hair. The company announced a contest asking girls to wear their hair like Shirley and submit their pictures, but some of the examples were frightful. Some Ideal dolls came with miniature Vassar curlers.

By early 1935, the films, the dolls, and Shirley had become big business. Shirley's increased earnings enabled the Temples to move to a larger house in Santa Monica. Instead of a wide open front lawn that was frequently trampled by eager fans, now Shirley had two secluded play areas. At that time, older brother Jack was learning film production and younger brother Sonny was enrolled in military school.

Shirley received gifts from fans on an ongoing basis, and these were frequently forwarded unopened to organizations for needy children. However, presents from studio staff had to be accepted, appreciated, and stored. Pets—perhaps inspired by several delightful photo series of Shirley with animals—were a frequent gift. Two wallabies were sent from Australia, but after a few roundups the fence-jumpers were transferred to a zoo, no doubt with a donation towards upkeep. Still, Shirley's publicists worked constantly to develop new photo ideas. The print media continually clamored for more Shirley pictures, whether newsworthy or just pure fun. The fact is that the photos sold magazines and newspapers.

Shirley could no longer enjoy playing at Santa Monica beach without being mobbed, and for that very reason she even had to give up Sunday school. Ordinary store shopping was also curtailed after a woman approached her and actually cut off a curl. Some hair, an autograph, a glimpse—everyone wanted a piece of Shirley's fame. Her parents screened requests, while her first-grade studio teacher, Frances Klamt, used films and visitors to create learning experiences. A visiting foreigner became a springboard for study of the person's country of origin. A politician or other individual of influence provided Miss Klamt with the opportunity to introduce Shirley to a world as yet unknown to her. Equally important, she also made sure that California schooling regulations were strictly adhered to.

When *The Little Colonel* went into production, every group that had colonels as officers or members wanted Shirley to "share" with them. The governor of Kentucky anointed her a colonel along with quite a few

Shirley was determined to keep all the pups in the basket. The photographer wants "just one more," after Shirley wants to quit.

The Saalfield Publishing Company's Shirley Temple and Her Playhouse *was published in the United States in 1935 and distributed worldwide. This book, sold in Denmark, carried Danish assembly instructions glued over the English.*

film stars and other people of note. Not far behind was the Hollywood Post of the American Legion, which made Shirley an honorary colonel, a commission that would be recognized by other posts. All of the attendant publicity helped exploit the film, so the studio pressbook urged theaters to contact any local Legion group to arrange mention in local newspapers, stage a parade, or even organize a party to view the film. The National Guard made Shirley a colonel, which applied to encampments in Idaho, Kansas, Kentucky, and New Jersey. Some of Shirley's popularity and box-office draw was the result of very crass commercialism, but audiences were not disappointed with Shirley the person or Shirley the movie star.

In 1934, the Saalfield Publishing Company had issued its first paper-doll book of Shirley, and it sold over one million copies. Additional paper dolls, coloring books, picture books, and tablets followed. Thick four-inch-square Big Little books as well as a variety of paperback and hardcover books featuring photos or careful likenesses of Shirley were available to delighted fans.

(Left) Shirley was made a colonel in the American Legion, Hollywood Post, with a commission dated January 26, 1935. Hanging over the top of the certificate is her medal. She wears the first of several Legion caps that she was to receive.

(Above) Colorado's 157th Infantry regiment of the National Guard made Shirley a Little Colonel. She dutifully posed, and the photo back got the Advertising Council stamp of approval, dated March 2, 1935.

(Left) Shirley was due for a vaccination by her doctor, Russell Sands, who had been caring for her since she was five months old. More than a photo opportunity, this was also a chance to encourage families to give their children similar protection. Shirley is relaxed before the camera. Dr. Sands is definitely ill-at-ease.

IN 1935, SHIRLEY WAS the big moneymaker in films. She helped save Fox from bankruptcy, and her films brought employment to many other players and production crews. Not only did each Shirley film require its own technicians, but the showings were accompanied by short subjects, including cartoons and news. Things were looking up for Hollywood, and somehow the industry had to salute the cause. The solution was to create a special Oscar to present at that year's Academy Awards ceremony that would recognize the previous year's outstanding work. There seems to have been no putdown intended by presenting Shirley with a small statuette, though the politics and egos of Hollywood may have made that a necessity. At any rate, on February 27, l935, Shirley was presented with her Oscar by Irvin S. Cobb.

Cobb said in part:

Darling, when Santa Claus bundled you up, a fragrant, delicious, dimpling, joyous doll-baby package, and dropped you down Creation's chimney, he gave to mankind the dearest and the sweetest Christmas present that ever gladdened the hearts and stirred the souls of this weary old world. Through your instinctive art and your natural artistry, millions and millions of children have been made to laugh and millions of older folks have laughed with them.

Then, with the typical adult attitude towards Shirley, he took her in his arms and asked for a kiss. She thanked everyone with few words—and he got his kiss.

(Top) Shirley receives a miniature Oscar for her 1934 contribution to the film industry. The presentation began on February 27, 1935, but it was nearly 1:00 A.M. before Irvin S. Cobb made his speech. Shirley looks a bit drowsy.

(Bottom) Then Cobb picked her up and wanted a kiss, and all the camera flashes went wild. Shirley knew it was time to sparkle, then she asked if it was time to go home.

The Academy of Motion Picture Arts and Sciences was correct in recognizing Shirley's contributions. She was very rapidly becoming a legend, and separating fact from the myth that surrounds any legend is difficult. In a 1934 article, Mrs. Temple wrote that Shirley was taught to be confident—so she wasn't afraid, not even of the rear-

> Portraits of Shirley were not always true-to-life. Magazine artists painted Shirley with blue eyes more often than brown. One "natural color cover" even produced green eyes to match a green coat. Plainly, almost from the start, people saw Shirley in very different ways.
>
> In a time when beauty, neatness, honesty, and religion were admired, Shirley publicity naturally emphasized them all. Patricia Hill, writing for a British fan magazine, commented, "It is no exaggeration to say that Shirley's charm has done as much to lift the world out of depression, by lightening the hearts of all who see her, as any of the wordy conferences that have been held by statesmen all over the world." Was that fabrication, or was it an honest appraisal of the ineffectiveness of politicians?

ing horse in *Little Miss Marker*. Frequently, as a film character, Shirley would announce that she was self-reliant. But as one account had it, during *Curly Top* filming it took three days to persuade Shirley to tap dance on the piano then fling herself into the waiting arms of John Boles.

Shirley Temple greatly influenced the world around her. A reviewer named Cameron described Shirley at Radio City Music Hall in *Bright Eyes* as the "sparkling Christmas ornament topping a Christmas pudding." In Portland, Oregon, the popularity of a typical Shirley film was joyously reported in *Film Daily*: "*Bright Eyes* broke all Christmas Day records at the Paramount with a take of $2,500." During the showing of *Curly Top* at New York's Music Hall, management had to stop

selling tickets several times during the day while long lines of fans waited to get in. Preliminary estimates put the week's income at over $90,000, with a possible holdover considered.

The Little Colonel premièred on March 14, 1935, and by that April six-year-old (studio age) Shirley had her own secretary. One room at the rear of the Temple family's second Santa Monica house was set aside for Shirley's fan mail and secretary. Letters were brought in daily by truck. Most mail was answered frequently with a card explaining that a photograph would be forwarded upon receipt of a dime to cover the cost.

To fulfill fan requests and accommodate publicity needs, Shirley posed for an average of twenty photos a day. This took at least an hour, which the youngster for the most part patiently endured. At one time as many as ten secretaries were employed at Fox to deal with the letters and gifts that poured in for Shirley, frequently as many as ten thousand a week. In hopes of discovering a rival treasure, other studios wrote scenes for children into their films. General Casting Office in Hollywood increased its listing of child players to one thousand five hundred.

Although the casts and production staffs with which Shirley worked were forbidden to praise her, they demonstrated their appreciation and friendship in many other ways. Because Shirley was curious, careful, and good-mannered (even when her mother wasn't nearby), they delighted in showing her how equipment worked. So she learned about the various lights, the sound system, cameras—anything that intrigued her.

Writers continually sought out news about Shirley, for just a short blurb in a column would bring sure cash and might open the door to bigger things. In fact, *Screen Book Magazine* of June 1935 went so far as to publish Shirley's weekly menu, prepared by baby specialist Dr. Russell Sands. It included spinach four days a week. Those were the days of Popeye, but most children hated spinach. That would have been all right except that nutrition was emerging as an issue of motherly concern, and spinach was declared desirable. Shirley was reported to love the leafy green vegetable, or evidently was forced to consume a great deal of it. One day she hatched a plot with the

(continued on page 44)

Photographers weren't content to give fans a sweet, ladylike impression of Shirley. By March 6, the Los Angeles wire service was sending out this tomboy pose. Notice: Shirley's entire outfit is new except for the shoes.

Shirley expressed her own generous feelings toward the world when she signed the cement at Grauman's Chinese Theatre using big printed letters: LOVE TO YOU ALL, SHIRLEY TEMPLE. She usually signed autographs with that same expression of love. She once explained why: "I can't sign them 'Your friend' because I don't even know them. But since I love everybody, it is telling the truth to sign them 'Love, Shirley Temple.'"

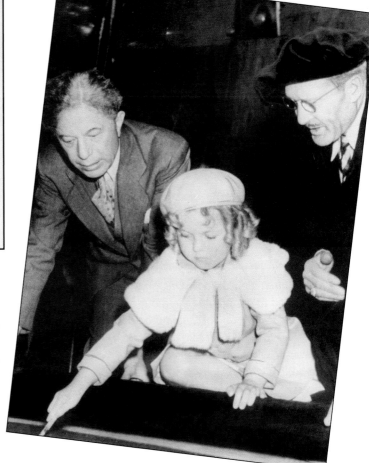

Shirley put her handprints and footprints into the cement at Grauman's Chinese Theatre as Sid Grauman (to her right) and Jean Klossner (to her left) look on. Shirley's mouth was tightly shut for all photos, as she had just lost a tooth.

Alberto Vargas was already famous for drawing sensuous ladies and later became well known for his pinup art. Here he works in pastels, and the Shirley portrait is nothing like his commissary art. It isn't even a good likeness.

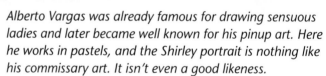

The children of Tillamook, Oregon, were persuaded to donate money to buy a calf as a gift for Shirley. She accepted graciously but soon had to send it off to a dairy farm. It was actually an advertising effort to promote Tillamook dairy products, especially cheese.

A Shetland pony, given by Joseph Schenck, came from Britain with a guardian. It became part of Shirley's private menagerie, even appearing in a film. Although many valuable or rare gifts had to be returned others were turned over to various charities. As though aware of her good fortune, by 1936 some fans were writing Shirley and asking for gifts of dolls instead of photos.

True Story

TRUTH IS STRANGER THAN FICTION

MAGAZINE

APRIL

15¢

A MACFADDEN PUBLICATION

SHIRLEY TEMPLE'S OWN STORY

TOLD by HER MOTHER

Bernarr [sic] Macfadden published many movie magazines. This painting of Shirley made the cover of his soap-opera-oriented True Story *magazine for April 1935. The story of Shirley as told by her mother joined other confessions inside. Notice that an artist so careful with curls and dress pleats got Shirley's eye color incorrect.*

Our Little Girl director John Robertson finds Shirley relaxing with the script in the shadow of some very heavy camera equipment.

Shooting on location at Sherwood Lake, "our little girl," looking rather cautious, sits astride a motorcycle belonging to the California Highway Patrol.

commissary staff: Mrs. Temple was served a plateful of spinach instead of her ordered lunch. A joyous Shirley announced that her mom had to eat it all—and was even inclined to help shove it in.

SHIRLEY LEARNED TO BE relaxed and cordial no matter what the gift or who the visitor. When H.G. Wells showed up, Shirley asked who he was. Mrs. Temple replied, "He's one of the most important men in the world." Shirley was silent for a moment, then disagreed. "Oh, but he can't be. There's God . . . and there's [director] David Butler."

Gertrude Temple and Shirley's teachers—first Miss Barkley then Miss Klamt—made sure to prepare Shirley to greet an expected visitor or graciously accept a gift. When Colonel Joseph Wolfson of the Philippines brought her a lovely handmade embroidered dress and woven hat, Shirley needed to know about fine embroidery, hat

Shirley, the doll bed, and the doll are cute, but director John Robertson doesn't dare look stern or "our little girl" will lose her happy smile. This is just pretend play.

uses, and the Philippines' famous pinya cloth, made from pineapple fiber. In anticipation of a visit by the prince of Siam, she needed to become familiar with the customs of that Asian land. To prepare for a visit by the crew of a cruiser, she would have to learn officer rankings and plan a suitable gift of her own.

Adults indulged Shirley. She and Jane Withers had competed for the showy imported doll Pinky

Studios sometimes spread less than accurate publicity. For example, the *Our Little Girl* props included a wooden doll bed. Shirley posed in the bed, tucked in, with one of the latest doll gifts placed on top. The studio released the photo with this caption mimeographed on the back: "Director John Robertson is trying to find out why Shirley Temple is in the doll's bed instead of working before the camera in *Our Little Girl*, her new picture for Fox Film. The doll is almost as big as Shirley." Shirley had no need of such rubbish publicity. The doll is in no way near her size, and when the cameras were ready for her, she was ready for them.

Will Rogers, who had helped on the story of *Stand Up and Cheer*, was Shirley's friend and bungalow neighbor on the old Fox lot. At the bungalow, Shirley reportedly kept a diary—perhaps as a school assignment—in which she recorded some noteworthy happenings, including a carefully written reference about wanting to make a picture with Will.

The closest Shirley came to actually working with Will Rogers was the day after the Grauman's première, when Will pulled the cord to unveil a portrait of Shirley in the Fox commissary. Noting that the real Shirley was not smiling, he tried to cheer her up. She confided about her missing tooth, and he assured her that he had experienced something similar. Later, she posed for pictures with a false tooth filling the gap, a technique she would take advantage of more than once.

In the summer, Shirley kept a Hawaiian diary, which later became a fan magazine feature, a contest prize, and a softcover picture book issued by Saalfield Publishing Company.

Prince Purachatra was said to have come all the way from Siam just to visit Shirley at the Fox Film Studio. An ardent amateur movie fan, he showed her several reels he had filmed of an elephant hunt.

during the filming of *Bright Eyes*. Jane, as the rich girl, got the doll in the film and seems to have monopolized it off-camera, bringing out rivalry, even covetousness, in Shirley. Director Winfield Sheehan noticed and gave the doll to Shirley. *Curly Top* publicity showed the doll decorating Shirley's bed. She also received several dolls handmade by Irving Cummings, her new director. This provided publicity opportunities for other Shirley Temple dolls.

While work was finishing up on *Curly Top*, the Temple family began to plan a trip to Hawaii. Fox finalized a merger with Twentieth Century, and Darryl F. Zanuck took over as studio head. The whole Temple family sailed for Hawaii on the *S.S. Maiposa* on July 24, 1935, looking forward to a relaxing month-long stay. Janet Gaynor, also a top Fox star, sailed a few days later and met up with Shirley, briefly commenting, "She was literally

mobbed every time she stepped out of the hotel in Honolulu." Will Rogers also took off from Fox for a trip to Arizona, so all the top Foxes were away from the den.

Shirley was allowed a brief turn at the *Maiposa*'s wheel and enjoyed a bit of time with her brothers. She sang her "Lollipop" song for crowds and graciously met shy native children to exchange leis and smiles. Crowds broke down barriers and mobbed police, trying to reach her. Others managed to get closer at private gatherings or by bringing gifts. Shirley collected a surfboard, hula outfit, ship souvenirs, and some wonderful dolls.

When Mrs. Temple announced that Shirley would visit Hawaii in the summer of 1935, a Japanese motion picture club based there asked children to contribute ten cents each to raise $2,000 for the commission and purchase of a Japanese bride doll to present to her. The funds were quickly

(continued on page 51)

The officers of the British cruiser H.M.S. Danae *visited Shirley en masse. They presented her with a British seaman's hat, and in return she gave them a terrier pup—fox, of course. Lucky, the dog, is asleep on the commander's lap, giving us some idea of how long the visit and posing lasted.*

Shirley also did some visiting. Here, on the set of Dick Powell's film Thanks a Million, *she meets violinist Rubinoff. He lets her help hold his $100,000 violin—and smiles.*

Ideal issued licenses to overseas firms wishing to make dolls using Shirley's name and likeness. First is Ideal's, with pin. Next is an all-cloth doll whose mask face is almost a grimace. The doll in stripes is made of felt; it has a much nicer face but too much hair and leg fat. The doll in the coin-dot dress is a typical-quality European make with ball-jointed limbs. Last is a lovely doll with a Spanish-text pin identifying it as "the little star of cinema, club of admirers."

(Right) This fine composition doll from Poland stands twelve inches high. The blonde bangs are curled, but the bonnet covers only waves leading to a roll of hair at the neck back. The clothes are original, including a full slip and separate panties. She has six teeth and eyes that blend blue and hazel. The head back is marked with a triangle and "Shirley Temple, Poland."

(Opposite, top left) Shirley's doll Pinky, made by the Italian firm Lenci, decorates her bed.

(Opposite, top right) Ideal created a large composition doll, dressed to match Shirley's Curly Top *caped dress and hat.*

(Opposite, bottom) A lineup of Ideal Shirley dolls shows variations in eyes and mouths as well as size. All have sleep eyes, but the largest also shows Ideal's latest innovation—flirting eyes that also move to the side.

49

Visitors to Hawaii traditionally learn the hula, so Shirley did her best. Later, picture spreads detailed a good dozen how-to poses.

Shirley was made a captain in the Beach Patrol and received a surfboard from Hawaiian swimming champion Pua Kealoha and beach patrolman Sally Hale. By the time Shirley left, she had lots of autographs on the surfboard.

(Right) Shirley's Japanese bride doll was larger than life. Below it are doll gifts from a ballet dancer and the Madame Alexander Doll Company.

(Below) Studio photographer Otto Dyar immediately photographed Shirley wearing the kimono given by the geisha girls. Six poses were rushed for approval, getting a September 4 date.

raised, and an artist began making the six-foot-tall representation. The head, complete with real hair, was made of porcelain; the rest of the doll was wood. It wore an authentic expensive kimono and beaten silver jewelry and held a delicate fan. Placed in Shirley's hotel room as a surprise, the doll was instead a shocking scare at first. Shirley carefully posed with it and her other doll gifts. It was more fun, however, to show off the special kimono that had been presented by Honolulu's geisha girls.

Even on vacation, Shirley had an obligation to consider people with special needs. She and her mother made a private visit to a badly burned girl at Schofield Barracks, home of many Pearl Harbor military people. It was there that the first news came through: WILEY POST AND WILL ROGERS CRASH NEAR BARROW, ALASKA. A check confirmed that both were dead. Shirley felt the loss deeply.

Twentieth Century–Fox hoped for great—

After Shirley had been piped aboard the U.S.S. Gamble at Pearl Harbor, the officers of the ship gave her a silver and engraved pipe. The sailors also presented her with a souvenir emblem pillow.

and cheap—publicity benefits from the Hawaii visit. Now, the need for profits was great. Shirley returned to Hollywood to begin preparation for *The Littlest Rebel*. This reunited her with the director reputed to be her favorite, David Butler, who was inclined to indulge his star. He had a stable of three horses and knew about racing, so he gave Shirley gear for her pony. Perhaps more exciting, he promised to name his next filly after her.

Following the special opening of *The Littlest Rebel* at Radio City Music Hall in December 1935 and its general release in January 1936, fan support was especially needed. Although the story was a good one, some critics objected to scenes in which Shirley and black actor Bill Robinson held hands. Many couldn't accept that the two had actually long been good friends.

When filming of *The Littlest Rebel* was complete, Darryl F. Zanuck gave Shirley a portable dressing room. He decorated the outside, and director David Butler furnished the inside with its own dressing table and nap couch. Zanuck also assigned his

friend John Griffith to be Shirley's bodyguard and driver. In time, Shirley and Grif became good friends. John's wife, Mabel, became Gertrude's maid, and John and Mabel kept a careful scrapbook of photos, mementos, and notes from Shirley.

When, on November 15, 1935, Twentieth Century-Fox dedicated a new sound stage that had been built in honor of Will Rogers, the governor of California and many other dignitaries were present to make speeches. Shirley certainly remembered sharing the spotlight with Will as he pulled the cord to unveil her portrait in the old Fox commissary. Now it fell upon her to pull the cord that would reveal Will's memorial portrait and plaque. Shirley's words were probably the most sincere spoken that day. "I loved him, too," she said as she removed the cover.

The new sound stage was put into use for the first time when Shirley filmed

A column of May 13, 1935, had Shirley in her own cursive writing give the recipe for how her mother prepared the delicious spinach, and it seemed too good a publicity angle to let drop. *Poor Little Rich Girl* featured a whole song urging, "You gotta eat your spinach, baby," this time with Shirley as a protester. The frequently cool British press, which generally objected to child players on principle, only gradually thawed to Shirley, while commoners had gone wild long before. Shirley's spiritual-style ending to the spinach song brought enthusiastic praise at last from *Film Weekly*'s reviewer.

(Right) Director David Butler gave Shirley a monogrammed blanket and feedbag for her pony. Then, he helped her demonstrate how to use them.

(Below) Fashion poses such as this in the Captain January *opera frock enticed audiences. It was especially important, since much of the film had Shirley in sailor pants.*

Captain January in early 1936. The huge warehouse structure was fitted with an eighty-foot-square waterfront and pool set to serve as a fishing port. It had a capacity of 143,616 gallons and could accommodate two full-rigged fishing boats plus a Coast Guard cutter. Workmen on three sides operated agitators that made waves. Vaporized mineral oil was cooled over dry ice to create low-hanging fog over the water.

Out went Shirley for the boat scenes. She had survived the long trip to and from the Hawaiian Islands, but on the Fox pond she became seasick. Shooting had to be postponed.

Coping with Stardom

Many minor incidents that occurred during shooting give glimpses into Shirley's personality and her attempts and frustration at coping in a very serious business. Amid confusion and boredom, she had to remain cooperative.

Shirley created her own games, some with precise rules. Sometimes Booth McCracken, an assistant director, would call Shirley to a scene but first be asked to circle her dressing room, count to ten, or be tied to a chair before work could begin. On the *Dimples* set, handcuffs substituted for the tying up. Perhaps Shirley was retaliating for constantly being ordered about. At last, she wanted to be in charge.

Shirley would often explore the set or beyond and hide in little enchanting nooks. Mrs. Temple had found other ways to spend her time, especially since her

THE TEMPLERS

SCREEN PLAY'S International SHIRLEY TEMPLE CLUB

CONDUCTED BY MRS. HARMONY HAYNES WOODWARD

Let's Celebrate Shirley's Birthday

EVER since Shirley Temple became a motion picture star, she has celebrated her birthday by inviting several hundred children to a party in the beautiful *Cafe de Paris on the Twentieth Century-Fox Lot*.

The party begins with games and ends with ice cream and a generous slice of the huge birthday cake. And you'd think it was everyone's birthday except Shirley's as you watch her handing out gifts and prizes, not to mention a lovely autographed photo of herself, to every little guest.

Shirley would like to invite every girl and boy in the world to her party this year, but, of course, that's impossible. However, you can all help her celebrate her birthday by joining *The Templers*.

Have a Shirley Temple Birthday Party of Your Own!

You better take Mamma in on these plans because you may need her help. Invite all your friends to your house for a Shirley Temple Birthday Party and while they are there ask them to join *The Templers!* Organize a sister club on Shirley's birthday and see if you cannot win a prize.

Remember! There are prizes and surprises for every *Templer* and a chance to become *President of The Templers*.

And don't forget to collect ten cents from every one who wishes to become a *Templer* to cover postage on the beautiful certificate of membership which SCREEN PLAY will forward to them.

Kathleen Anne Pape of Macon, Ga., aged six. She sings and dances. SCREEN PLAY is showing her picture to producers. She may get a screen contract. Send in your photos, too

Shirley has lunch with the May Templer president—Noel Oliver, aged 5, of Los Angeles, Calif. Each month a new president is chosen

Be Our June TEMPLER President!

IT'S a cinch, boys and girls! All you have to do is send in the largest number of new *Templers* during the coming month.

School isn't out yet so you have a wonderful chance to talk things over with the boys and girls in your neighborhood. Ask them to join *The Templers* and to give you credit for their membership.

The boy or girl sending us the largest number of new *Templers* is elected *President of the Templers* for the month of June and has his or her picture printed in SCREEN PLAY. In addition to that honor, Shirley will send the new President an autographed photo of herself.

Rules of the Club

THE membership fee to join *The Templers* is only ten cents. There are no other fees or charges of any kind, but there are rules which must be followed if a *Templer* wishes to be an official brother or sister of little Shirley Temple.

Shirley is one of the best behaved and nicest little girls imaginable, and she hopes that all of the members of her club will follow the rules of conduct her mother outlines for her.

The rules are simple but they are important. Shirley follows them and wants every *Templer* to do the same.

RULES

To obey promptly.
To be clean and neat.
To study faithfully.
To be kind and thoughtful.
To be thrifty.

Send in Your Photos

ONE of the purposes of *The Templers* is to help the motion picture producers find talented children for the screen.

Accompanying every certificate of membership in *The Templers*, will be a "talent coupon." Fill in the coupon, attach it to your photo and forward it to SCREEN PLAY offices in Hollywood.

If in the opinion of the SCREEN PLAY executives, you look like a screen find, your photo will be presented to Hollywood producers.

You need not have a picture taken especially for this purpose. A snap shot will do just as well. In fact, often producers would rather have a snap shot because it looks more natural, and naturalness is what counts on the screen.

If you doubt this, just watch Shirley Temple on the screen. Isn't she so natural that you feel as if she is right in the room with you? It has been said of Shirley that she never acts at all.

Too many children over-act. Producers do not like this. They call it "posing" and posing it is. A child who is always putting on an act for the producer never is the child chosen for the part.

Maybe you recall the story of the little boy who was being given a screen test and acting very naughty about it. The producer finally asked, "Don't you want to go to Hollywood?" The little boy replied, "Naw, but my Mamma does."

That little boy was being himself and the director was so pleased he gave him the part.

Incidentally, in suggesting you send in photographs, SCREEN PLAY wishes it understood that no pictures can be returned.

Entry Blank

To the Templers,
SCREEN PLAY Magazine,
7046 Hollywood Boulevard,
Hollywood, California.

I promise to follow all the rules of *The Templers*, and wish to enroll. Please send me my Certificate of Membership. To cover expense of certificate and mailing I enclose ten cents.

Name ....Age ....

Address ....

City ....

State ....

In May 1936, The Templers' newsletter showed that month's president lunching with Shirley.

longtime friend was the mother of Shirley's stand-in, Mary Lou Isleib. Gertrude's absence gave Shirley a bit less of the watchful eye, but she was always somewhat indulged by the adult stars and the crews, and this sometimes became problematic. When still photographer Anthony Ugrin married, Shirley was hurt, feeling that Anthony no longer loved her as he had effusively declared. Adults didn't always mean what they said, but Shirley did. If prop man Eddie Jones, aka Jonesy, moved the portable dressing room and she wasn't inside for the ride, Shirley would keep him in the doghouse for hours—that is, she would no longer ask him for favors. Instead of feeling relieved, Jonsey would be hurt.

Although cast and crew were instructed not to fawn over the young star, she was frequently the center of attention, and they felt her slights as keenly as she did those of her photographer. When

(Above) Two photos were shot within minutes. One with Shirley puzzling at the typewriter was widely published. This is the real scene: Bill Robinson was working on his autobiography, Tap Dancer, *and pal Shirley came to watch, then read over his shoulder.*

(Left) It was reported that the thousands of fan letters Shirley received each week required secretaries to answer them. A close look shows that this stack of mail all came from a promotion in Des Moines, Iowa's Register and Tribune. *Shirley's name drummed up more business for the paper than any star ever had.*

Shirley publicized various mail and communications systems. Here, in an outfit from The Poor Little Rich Girl, *she promoted the use of the Postal Telegraph services.*

a problem arose in Mrs. Temple's presence, a look from Mom was usually enough to establish calm. It wasn't a "Wait till you get home!" sort of glance, but at least as effective. Shirley understood the difference between work and play—and she knew her place.

Shirley's vocabulary was reported to be 750 words (that of the average adult was said to be about 450), and a serious attempt was made not

There had been countless local Shirley Temple fan clubs and even one organized by a movie magazine. *Screen Play's* club, The Templers, got a studio visit with the star. The club promoted good behavior and star admiration, but also suggested the possibility that any member might be chosen for a film part. Twentieth Century-Fox gladly supported every promotion angle.

to add to it by exposing her to obscene language, a challenge considering that Shirley had two very sharp ears. On the *Captain January* set, a parrot was returned to the trainer because it had the so-called "language of a sea dog." Director Butler declared with great relief, "Good thing we got the parrot here early enough in the day before Shirley's mother arrived on the set with her, so we could get acquainted with his vocabulary!" Mrs. Temple's influence reached far beyond her child.

The Mystique Grows

Studio publicists continued to idealize Shirley through words and pictures. Friends and relatives of the studio staff as well as the famous and near-famous came to pose with her regularly. Director Irving Cummings brought his football-star son, who in turn brought his university coach. It was as though being near Shirley Temple would insure that a bit of her good fortune would rub off.

Some were convinced that resembling Shirley physically might bring success their way. Doting

Studio publicity claimed this to be Shirley's favorite doll, although it was not and never appeared again. Some writers said the doll was from Gertrude's childhood and served as her inspiration for Shirley's curls.

mothers wanted their children to be Shirley clones, and beauty shops carried posters of the Shirley Temple hairstyle along with diagrams showing how the style could be copied.

Shirley's fans also liked to copy her film mannerisms. There were talent shows in which children would sing or dance in Shirley manner, and there were even lookalike contests. Some children loved it and, as adults, still are fans. Others hated it and continue to resent Shirley. As though hoping to bridge the gap, in *Child Star* Shirley seems to delight in bursting that paragon-of-virtue bubble by showing glimpses of the childhood "fiendishness." Most likely, she is simply trying to reveal the real person beneath the hype.

Gertrude tried to maintain a balance in Shirley's life and keep her ego in check. She explained that people came because they were curious, or cared, or because she made them happy. Studio heads were more blunt: The more often important people came to visit Shirley, the more publicity resulted, and the more the world was able to see that she was still an adorable little child. That added up to larger grosses for Shirley's films. A tug of war was developing as studio interests wanted to keep Shirley "a child" while Gertrude sought to let her daughter mature naturally. Those who came to visit—or sent gifts—sided with the studio.

Much of the Shirley publicity was contrived. In 1936, the Twentieth Century-Fox public relations department arranged for a group of Southern California Eagle Scouts to be honored at the studio. As part of the gala day, the scouts had lunch with Shirley and posed with her holding the badge of one saluting scout. Uniforms varied widely, but facial expressions did not.

Studio releases proclaimed Shirley to be a child prodigy, a genius. Psychologists who tested her to determine mental capacity (and gain personal publicity) concluded that she was indeed bright, but not a prodigy. In January 1936 *Screen Play* published Shirley's IQ as 155, with 135 being the score for a genius and 100 the average, but this was based on an incorrectly given age, one year less than she really was.

Shirley was certainly attuned to her surroundings. Once, when a columnist visited her bungalow at Twentieth Century-Fox and interviewed Mrs. Temple about her daughter's preferences and diet, it was assumed from her quiet play that Shirley was unaware of the interview. Then, suddenly, she chimed in: "Why don't you ask me? *I'm* the star."

(Top left) Another chance to look like Shirley, this blue pleated frock from Stowaway was presumably designed by Royer and copied by Cinderella to promote both the film and dress sales.

(Top right) An unusual profile pose made by glamour photographer Hurrell features Stowaway, Shirley's beauty, and the tie-up clothes.

(Bottom left) A Cinderella dress was offered in the same style. The hat, gloves, and bag came from other manufacturers, but always with the GENUINE SHIRLEY TEMPLE label.

The scouts plainly were *not* thrilled, but Mrs. Frank Merriam, wife of the state's governor, was. Studio hype described her as "Shirley's guest." Supposedly, this was to become an annual event, with the next year bringing some two hundred Eagles from all over the state to descend on the studio for an encampment. There is no documentation that another event of this type ever took place.

In the summer of 1936, the Temples took

(Above) The Eagle Scouts of Southern California gathered at the studio to be honored by Shirley. The governor's wife, Mrs. Frank P. Merriam, and one boy look happy. The twenty-five scouts are there, but where are the scoutmasters?

(Right) Actually, Shirley was a Campfire Girl. Building a twig cabin at home is a great project. There's no younger child to get in the way, but her dog, Ching-Ching, makes up for that!

a vacation trip up the West Coast. At Grants Pass, Oregon, Shirley was made an honorary caveman. In Washington, she toured Mount Rainier National Park, then headed north across the border for salmon fishing and tours of British Columbia. With Grif as Shirley's bodyguard, the crowds seemed less of a hazard, but they tended to shove Mr. and Mrs. Temple out of the way to concentrate on Shirley. This trip got a brief mention in *Life* magazine, while newsreels, especially *Fox Movietone News*, gave coverage in theaters.

59

(Left) In her satin Stowaway pajamas, Shirley admires this metal stove for Christmas, an exact model of a pre-1900 range, which would burn real wood. The chimney is great—but ban the wood!

(Below left) In this costume tryout for Wee Willie Winkie, a young lady, not a cute kid, is emerging.

(Below) Before Thanksgiving, Shirley donned a brief dance suit and became the New Year 1937 to a departing skinny old 1936, to be released on December 28. So confusing for her to keep track of time, yet such a message of cheer!

This color portrait appeared in the Chicago Sunday Tribune *on November 1, 1936. Good printing certainly brings out the skin tones and hair highlights, but it also shows the rouge, lipstick, and eyeliner.*

One of several Shirley Temple Scrap Book *items from the Saalfield Publishing Company, it featured the latest* Captain January *photo cover but was published just in time for this* Stowaway *publicity.*

(Left) During Stowaway, *someone presented Shirley with this spectacular tooled leather saddle. The artist's name wasn't given. Much later, when western fans tried to locate the treasure, Shirley said she thought her brother George had sold it to a friend.*

(Below) *At the February 1937 March of Dimes birthday party for President Roosevelt, Eddie Cantor shook Shirley's hand and wished her well before she cut the cake—and the President's head.*

Following vacation, it was back to work and back to business for those capitalizing on the Temple persona. Ideal held the exclusive license to make Shirley Temple dolls, with the studio receiving no financial remuneration. The dolls did not appear in Shirley films, perhaps because the licensing fee was too high. Whatever the reason, it is Effanbee dolls, not Ideal, that one sees in the films. Quite frequently, the hanging wrist tag heart, the emblem of the company, is plainly visible on dolls in *Bright Eyes*, *Curly Top*, and *Captain January*. The *Stowaway* Christmas scene features an assortment of popular toys. Special Christmas poses, tied to the season and seasonal release of a film, also featured dolls and toys. Many were very special.

Shirley continued with her schedule of making films, attending school, posing for photos, greeting visitors, and making public appearances. Despite studio efforts, photos often showed a young lady rather than a child. Among the visitors, there were a surprising number of Japanese, including diplomats with their children and even military groups. Japan seemed to have a special fascination with Shirley, and that has continued. In the mid-1990s a Shirley Temple specialty shop featuring little girl's frilly frocks, embroidered anklets, and other apparel bearing the Shirley name opened in Tokyo. Despite the high prices, sales were brisk.

Mrs. Seiziro Yoshizawa, wife of a Japanese diplomat, visited Shirley on the set of Wee Willie Winkie, *and her three children got to pose with Priscilla Williams Winkie as played by Shirley. The visitors were sailing for Tokyo on February 1, 1937.*

February of 1937 saw Shirley as guest of honor at the Los Angeles area March of Dimes fundraiser. It celebrated the birthday of President Franklin Delano Roosevelt, a polio victim, while soliciting money to help victims of that dreaded disease. That year Eddie Cantor was also a guest of honor, but it was Shirley who cut the cake. She wore the same dress she would wear a few months later for the première of *Wee Willie Winkie*.

Easter always meant special photo shoots. Perhaps it was a studio effort to further publicize their child star. Perhaps it was in anticipation of a church sequence planned for the upcoming *Heidi*. It might even have been out of a sincere religious feeling. At any rate, 1937 Easter poses ignored the eggs, bunnies, and chicks of previous years. The

photographer dressed Shirley in a lace surplice and had her sing or kneel before a stained-glass window. As if not soulful enough, one photo was retouched to add a halo. Nothing really was needed. The posing Shirley was sufficiently meditative.

Sometimes the public relations frenzy got to be too much even for pleasant-mannered Shirley. When her eighth birthday was to be celebrated at Twentieth Century-Fox's Café de Paree, one hundred fifty guests were invited—not her friends, but those the studio chose for payback or publicity. After years of cooperating, this year Shirley begged for no photographers to interrupt. It wouldn't be an enjoyable gala, but at least she wouldn't have to keep stopping to pose alone or with a guest. It was reported that over one thousand birthday cakes arrived as gifts. There was even one from the governor of Tennessee shaped like the state's capitol building. At least it didn't include his head!

Wee Willie Winkie was released in Great Britain in time for Christmas of 1937, as usual considerably behind domestic release. Of course, there had been plenty of publicity in the United States, and this quickly crossed the ocean. But the British wanted fresh items of their own. This time it was a lead feature in the December 25 issue of *Film Pictorial*: "SHIRLEY TEMPLE'S A GREAT KID!"

SAYS VICTOR MCLAGLEN. He was filming in Britain, so this story was local and the latest. McLaglen told how Shirley questioned the reality of his thrust-out chest, suspecting a pillow or board. Then, when director John Ford accused someone of bellowing like a water buffalo, Shirley wanted to know what the real thing sounded like. Vic and John got down on their knees to both posture and bellow in competition.

McLaglen had lots of stories to tell, because he and Shirley had spent nearly two months on location at the famous Iverson Movie Location Ranch, near Chatsworth, California. Shirley had a self-contained trailer and her father came up for frequent visits. McLaglen told of a scene where Shirley as Winkie had come home from sneaking flowers, with her clothes all wet and dirty. So totally unladylike! Producer Darryl Zanuck viewed the rushes and declared that the scolding she got just didn't ring true; there was no outrage. Mother Temple commented that any real mother would have given the child a spanking. Just the thing, except that actress June Lang as the mother had problems with that. She feared for her career if fans saw her spank the screen's idol. Shirley comforted her with, "Go ahead. I've had this before." This was accompanied, in McLaglen's account, by another water buffalo bellow.

The British magazine also contained a protest letter stating that if the British had banned child labor and the people supported the ban, then it should include Shirley. They ought not to excuse her, for surely if any child worked as

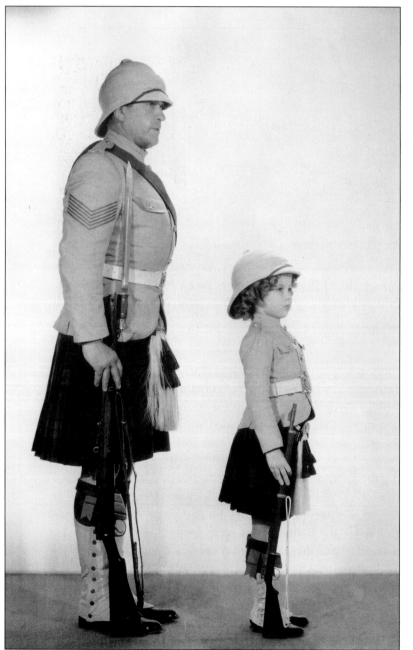

Barrel-chested Victor McLaglen and Shirley almost suggest Mutt and Jeff of the comics, but their authentic Black Watch kilts and dignified manner make it all proper.

hard as an adult star, it was she, and she had schoolwork besides. It was "slave labour," the writer declared. At least it included some of the same hazards for Shirley as for adults. On the set of *Wee Willie Winkie*, she had tripped over a light cord, pitched into a projector, and ended up with a black eye.

In the summer of 1937, after the release of *Wee Willie Winkie*, Shirley and company made a second trip to Hawaii. Brother George, who was involved in sports activities over the summer, passed up the trip. But Mabel and John Griffith were there, plus a doll named Jimmy, which Shirley seemed to genuinely fancy.

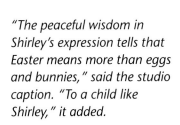

Shirley is proud of the black eye she got on the Winkie *set. Thanks to a news photo with date for release, one learns that this was rushed by wire on June 3, 1937.*

"The peaceful wisdom in Shirley's expression tells that Easter means more than eggs and bunnies," said the studio caption. "To a child like Shirley," it added.

(Above) Shirley says goodbye to big brother Jack in San Francisco. The kiss is the real thing.

(Top right) Brother George came aboard the Malolo to say goodbye. This time, he gets the kiss.

(Right) After a pose with her parents at the ship's railing, the photographer asked for Shirley alone. The paper retouched the photo accordingly, then decided to even touch up Shirley.

Back from Hawaii, Shirley welcomes a visitor more to her liking, Mary McArthur, daughter of Helen Hayes and Charles McArthur. Shirley has a great dollhouse complex to show off.

They set sail on the *Malolo* on August 5, and after a two-week stay on the island, returned home on the same ship. During a stopover in San Francisco, Shirley visited brother Jack, who was attending college.

Honolulu meant big crowds once more. Shirley was escorted off the ship on the shoulders of the sheriff, her old friend swimmer Duke Kahanamoku. She visited the estates of friends of her parents and swam in their private pools. She made assorted appearances, receiving various honors and gifts. She took photos at Schofield Barracks and Pearl Harbor, although such photos were strictly forbidden. But she didn't know and no one stopped her. A December 1937 *Movie Mirror* article about her visit, written by Kirtley Baskette, had a disconcerting opening: "News Flash. The Hawaiian Islands have been conquered! Pearl Harbor has fallen and Schofield Barracks has surrendered." The reference was to Shirley, of course. But four years later, another Temple, brother George, would be there not to sightsee the pride of the Pacific, but to face the reality of conquest.

After Hawaii, it was back to work to get *Heidi* ready for Christmas 1937 release. Immediately, Shirley received more distinguished visitors.

Irving Berlin and his daughter, Mary Ellin, visit Shirley on the set of Heidi. *How cool and comfortable Mary Ellin looks while Shirley wears at least four warm layers of clothes as she perches on the arm of director Allan Dwan's chair.*

This time, it was a McArthur and then the great composer Irving Berlin with his daughter, Mary Ellin.

Heidi had a lovely, long Christmas sequence, but it was filmed far ahead of the real season. However, after counting up her circle of friends, Shirley began making as many Christmas cards

Heidi gives Shirley another very tall leading man in Arthur Treacher. This Christmas scene emphasized the difference.

as she could. By beginning early in the film's shooting, she just might get the job done. The crew also knew just what she would be doing.

For *Heidi*, Shirley was dressed in some folk and period costumes. Two dream sequences gave her fancy outfits and two totally new hairstyles—in the form of wigs. First introduced to the press and public as a Dutch girl, she sported a very blonde hairdo with long looped-up braids and curled bangs. Then came the clincher: a high powdered wig and a gorgeous Marie Antoinette gown. It was a new, creative way to showcase Shirley, but was it inspired by the major film *Marie Antoinette*, released that year by another studio?

In addition to all the usual Santa and toy poses for Christmas, the 1937 holiday season had some-

The Dutch dance is a delightful dream sequence in Heidi, *and so is the hairdo.*

thing special for Shirley—the première of Walt Disney's feature-length cartoon *Snow White and the Seven Dwarfs*. On December 21, Shirley, two "girl friends," and her parents attended. Her real escorts were the seven dwarfs minus Snow White. One hopes the dwarfs didn't have to sit through the film in those head masks! Shirley would get to remove her ermine-trimmed coat.

Some unpleasant publicity began to surface in 1938 during the making of *Rebecca of Sunnybrook*

(continued on page 74)

As Marie Antoinette, Shirley is spectacular. The set design isn't half bad, either.

The Chicago Sunday Tribune *evidently saved this for a color cover, missing Valentine's Day by a week. The natural color film picks up Shirley's brown eyes beautifully, along with other details.*

Long before Roswell, New Mexico, made news with flying-saucer reports, its citizens sent Shirley a greeting celebrating *Rebecca of Sunnybrook Farm*. *Naturally, each person came to the theater to affix his or her signature.*

(Opposite, top left) Shirley attended the Disney première on December 21, 1937. This time, Gertrude and George were crowded out by kids and seven dwarfs. Talk about no respect!

(Opposite, top right) Wampas Baby Stars Shirley Temple and Gloria Stuart were reunited in Rebecca of Sunnybrook Farm. *This is one of many publicity portraits.*

(Opposite, bottom) This time, at the March of Dimes party, Shirley got a special confection portrait of herself.

(Right) Shirley welcomed an American Legion veteran and bought benefit tickets, graciously ignoring the fact that he was missing a leg. The setting was Rebecca.

(Left) Shortly after her ninth birthday, Shirley and her parents visited Palm Springs. Here, she and her father, George, enjoy a pleasant time pedaling along the bicycle path.

(Opposite) This pose with Ching-Ching was taken in May 1938. It was published in the following December's issue of Popular Photography, just one indication of why it is so hard to date photos precisely.

(Below) On June 16, Shirley was in Chicago. Scores of children and their mothers wanted to see her, but it is the newspeople who get to crowd close.

Farm. Along with other stars and many congressmen, Shirley was cited as a Communist dupe by a former member of the Communist Party. At the Dies Committee hearing on un-American activities, James B. Matthews charged that Temple, Gable, Cagney, and Robert Taylor had sent congratulations to the French newspaper *Ce Soir* on its publication anniversary. He maintained that the paper was owned by the Communists. The news report printed their defense: "The studios pointed out they are deluged with hundreds of requests every year from newspapers throughout the world for statements of greeting or congratulations."

With the Communist involvement in the Spanish civil war, those were serious charges, but they soon were turned down as groundless, especially after Matthews linked Roosevelt's New Deal to the Communists as well. Then, later in the year, an extortion letter and plot—death to Shirley if you don't pay—was traced to a boy sender in Portland, Oregon, but not before it terrified Mrs. Temple. The Lindbergh kidnapping and murder was followed by the Washington state kidnapping of the Wayerhaeuser boy, and Gertrude always worried that Shirley might be next.

In 1938, the March of Dimes celebration came on January 29. The official President's Ball, held at the Ambassador Hotel's Coconut Grove, featured Jay Whidden and his orchestra plus stars Tyrone Power and Don Ameche. The newspaper ad declared, "Shirley Temple will cut our birthday cake." She had to stand on a chair to do so. This was reported as her first nightclub visit, but not the first time she snitched frosting from the featured cake!

As usual, when convenient, Shirley spent time at Palm Springs, where so many other stars went to relax in semiprivacy. There were plenty of sports activities, though photos suggest that posing at poolside was fine for Shirley as long as she stayed out of the water to spare her hair. Part of the time, at least, she stabled her pony Roanie there.

Although Shirley did not travel far for public appearances, in the summer of 1938 fans across the U.S. finally had the opportunity to see her in person. It also gave Shirley's parents, bodyguard Grif, and his wife, Mabel, the chance to show her the country. All crowded into one car, and on May 31, 1938, they left Los Angeles for a cross-country trip.

Everywhere, photographers noted Shirley's activities. On June 12, she was at Pike's Peak, then she posed holding hands with a Grand Canyon National Park ranger. By June 16, she was interviewed in Chicago with her hair all properly acurl after some time tied up in kerchiefs.

The cover of *Life* magazine, July 11, 1938, shows Shirley in a Kansas wheat field. There was further coverage inside the magazine. The Swedish film magazine *Filmjournalen*, July 24, 1938, did an even better job with the same photo by using tones of orange and green on sepia brown on the cover.

WHEN THE TEMPLES stopped at Hays, Kansas, they secured motel rooms during a bad dust storm. In the morning, they awoke to another storm—that of people crowding, milling about, yet genuinely respectful. The throngs pulled back to make an aisle so that the family could reach a restaurant for breakfast. They just watched, proud and happy at the honor bestowed upon their town. A later visit to Hays by friends of the Temples brought Shirley the news that their table was still roped off and a framed menu of the day of the visit sat atop the table. This was the homage of ordinary people.

The party reached Washington, D.C., on June 23. The next day, curls properly done up, Shirley visited the Roosevelts, repaying a visit Mrs. Roosevelt had made to Shirley in Hollywood the previous March. As she left the White House on June 24, Mrs. Temple was smiling happily as Grif held back some of the crowd. An odd note on the back of a photo from the White House visit described Shirley as a redhead.

During the Washington stay, Shirley also got to visit FBI headquarters to satisfy her interest in police work, machine guns, even handcuffs. She covered her ears as her father and J. Edgar Hoover got off a few rounds at the FBI firing range. She had to let Hoover kiss her—a great deal less fun!

By July 2, the Temples were in New York City. Newspapers printed a photo on July 14 showing Shirley embarking on the *S.S. Queen of Bermuda*, carrying one of several dolls that made the trip

On June 24, Shirley visited the White House. Upon leaving, she was mobbed. Here, her mother smiles for the camera, Shirley waves goodbye, and bodyguard Grif, in the center, gently restrains the crowd.

with her. Grif stood beside her and Papa Temple, being unarmed, followed behind. In Bermuda on July 22, Vincent Astor led Shirley on an inspection of the Galapagos penguins. At Castle Harbour, she briefly drove the horse and carriage and squinted at the sun.

Back in New York once more, she posed showing where she had lost a lower tooth. Shirley arrived in Boston by August 1, a visit originally planned before Bermuda. The people anxiously awaited her, afraid they might be passed by. They had to exercise patience for several days because Shirley was in ill health; the flu, even malaria, was

Shirley's fascination with police work was indulged at FBI headquarters. A kiss from J. Edgar Hoover was just to be gotten over with.

suspected. Her personal physician, Dr. Leo Madsen, flew out from Santa Monica at Gertrude's request, but he would give no statement. Crowds waited outside the hotel and sent in greetings. A single photographer was allowed in to take and share photos of Shirley abed on the fourteenth floor of the Ritz-Carlton. Her 101-degree temperature climbed to 103, and the doctor was reported to be at her bedside all night, with a nurse also engaged. The final verdict: too much heat, excitement, and travel.

When Shirley was again up and about, she visited the Boston Public Gardens for a ride in its famous swan boats. While still ill, she had received a letter naming her "Admiral of the Swan Boat Navy." The crowds were almost overwhelming, and there were several near-accidents as fans crowded the steps by the water.

The Temples completed their Boston visit and headed home by train, arriving on August 7 in Pasadena, which was in the throes of a heat wave. Some in the crowd of about three thousand passed out. Again, as in Washington, D.C., comment was made about Shirley's red hair; evidently the touch-up bleach had not been used. Mr. Temple reported that Shirley's hand, slammed in a car door in Boston, was now thoroughly mended. The Temple entourage squeezed through the crowd to the car to drive home.

(Top) Shirley found the sun in Bermuda plenty bright, so she squints as she drives the horse-and-carriage at Castle Harbour.

(Left) On June 28, Shirley visited the mint. There, Secretary of the Treasury Henry Morgenthau presented her with a proof coin.

Crowds mobbed the Boston Public Gardens seeking a view of Shirley. People are looking in different directions, but right in the center at the water's edge is Grif, so Shirley must be close by.

(Right) On August 3, Shirley, once again in good health, enjoyed Boston's Swan Boats. Here is the admiral herself.

Shirley has just uncovered the Oscar display after her speech. She presents Oscar, leaving him safely on the table.

Late in October 1938, Shirley received an invitation to be Grand Marshal of the New Year's Rose Parade. She was the first child so chosen, though not the first film star, following legends such as Mary Pickford and Harold Lloyd. It was an even greater honor because this was the Rose Festival's Golden Jubilee. Since the new year started on Sunday, the parade was held on January 2. Shirley wore a long furlike coat with matching hat. A souvenir folder showed a view of her waving, but the group at curbside was small, with most looking elsewhere.

Shirley was chosen to present the Oscars for *Snow White* at the 1939 Academy Awards. There was the usual big Oscar for Best Picture, but there were also seven small ones. Shirley asked whether, since the big one was for filmmaker Walt Disney, there was also a small one for Snow White. In her

mind, she may have been comparing the dwarf Oscars to the miniature Oscar statuette she had received years before.

A Time of Transition

All was not well with Shirley's career. Ever since *Rebecca of Sunnybrook Farm*, the Temples had been concerned about Shirley's movie vehicles. They felt that *Rebecca* was incorrectly titled, misleading people to expect the beloved Kate Douglas Wiggin story. The only thing it had in common with the original was the farm, but as soon as Mrs. Temple raised an objection, recriminations began. Did the studio want to keep Shirley as just a song-and-dance girl? Several films said yes: *Rebecca of Sunnybrook Farm*, *Little Miss Broadway*, and *Just Around the*

Shirley is escorted from the ship to her hotel in Hawaii. The miniature parade was obviously unplanned, for people crowded between the usual parked cars to see her.

Corner. Did the Temples want more drama and storyline to showcase Shirley's talents? Then *Wee Willie Winkie* and *Heidi* did just that. *The Little Princess* drew its story from another childhood classic and added some Shirley song-and-dance plus drama, as though trying to please everyone.

What no one had factored in was the diminishing overseas market due to war. Distribution was smaller; so was income, and not just from foreign sources. Perhaps domestic audiences were less enchanted by the upbeat songs, dances, and happy endings of Shirley's movies. Yes, there was plenty of tragedy in her films: a mother killed, parents massacred, family missing due to unspecified

Shirley receives her Grand Marshal badge and bouquets of golden roses to officially begin the celebration leading to the New Year's Parade—and it was only November 28.

causes, and a father presumed dead though finally turning up only wounded. Meanwhile, radio news told of real war: bombings, bloodshed, pillage, massacres, terror, anguish. All over the country changes were happening as manufacturing moved from peacetime needs to help with Great Britain's war needs.

Meanwhile, the Temples made a third trip to Hawaii, sailing on the *Matsonia* on May 4, 1939. They saw old sites, including Schofield Barracks and military installations at Pearl Harbor, and they saw old friends, including Duke Kahanamoku. They saw the crowds from their motorcade and spent a busy six weeks, interrupted by only one bad moment when air-raid sirens were sounded for a test and Shirley went into near hysteria.

After Shirley completed *Susannah of the Mounties*, again a dramatic film based on another childhood classic, she was scheduled to start a film entitled *Lady Jane*, but Darryl Zanuck suddenly changed his mind. Perhaps influenced by news of *The Wizard of Oz*, he hoped for a knockout punch by filming Maeterlinck's great fantasy *The Blue Bird* instead. And he would shoot it all in Technicolor.

Zanuck had some work to get out of the way first. There was *Stanley and Livingstone*, which was just into sneak preview before any final editing. *The Rains Came* was nearly finished; *Hollywood Cavalcade* was half finished; and *The Grapes of Wrath* had just been purchased. As usual, Zanuck was thoroughly involved in most details of each film. He was also still dealing with the "Communist sympathizer" attacks. Into this fevered schedule came Maurice Cowan, a Fox executive from Great Britain.

Cowan had planned to come just for a holiday, but he was asked by Lord Southwood to see if he could arrange for Shirley to film an appeal. The Great Ormond Street Hospital for Children needed some 350,000 pounds. He wasn't asking Shirley for money; he was asking her to film a plea to the British to donate money for their hospital.

As Cowan reported in the British film magazine *Picturegoer* of September 16, 1939, busy studio head Zanuck still had time for him. Of course, as was proper, Cowan had made his approach through Roy Simmonds in the London office, then in Hollywood through Harry Brand and "Doc"

As the Matsonia *was returning to her berth in San Pedro, California, Captain Frank A. Johnson let Shirley take the wheel briefly. The news photo is dated June 15, 1939, 9:00 A.M.*

Bishop, who looked after the press. Zanuck promptly gave permission for Shirley to film the plea and placed studio space and staff at Cowan's disposal. Just one detail: get permission from Mrs. Temple. This called for a visit to Ray Dannenbaum, who acted as a sort of liaison officer between the studio and the Temples. Obviously, there was some careful stepping going on.

Shirley, her mother, and Cowan discussed the deal over lunch in Shirley's bungalow. Shirley asked about London—they still hoped to visit there next year—and about the hospital. All was agreed. Walter Lang, who had directed *The Little Princess*, was put at the helm, with Arthur Miller in charge of photography. Cowan and the studio prepared the script.

A scene from The Autograph Hound, *as reproduced in the Dutch magazine* Mickey Maanblad, *May 1978.*

Shirley's stand-in, Mary Lou Isleib, showed up and wore a long flannel nightgown not quite matching Shirley's. Shirley's complete crew was there, right down to the clapper-boy. Troy Orr was also there, the executive who would take charge of the finished film. There were two minor slip-ups during rehearsal when Shirley said "Armond" for "Ormond" and "shillins" for "shillings." But she got it right after that. Everyone on the set obviously adored her, Cowan reported. At the end, he offered her a souvenir shilling.

"Oh, no thank you," she replied. "I'm glad to make this film [appeal] for nothing. I don't expect to be paid," Cowan noted. He figured that her regular salary for the film would have been about 1,000 pounds.

SHIRLEY HAD MADE some other short appeals, most notably one for the Red Cross in 1936 entitled *For Their Sakes*. Dressed in a miniature nurse outfit, she urged people to give a dollar to help. Twentieth Century-Fox approved both this and the 1939 Great Ormond Street Hospital for Children Appeal.

Shirley also turned up in several films without any approval from her studio. In 1939 Walt Disney made *The Autograph Hound*, a cartoon in which a chubby young Shirley joined Disney characters. Leon Schlesinger put a cartoon Shirley in his Merrie Melodie titled *Hollywood Steps Out*, and while the date is uncertain, there is strong resemblance to the Disney caricature. A composite of three of the old Frolics of Youth comedies—collectively called "Our Girl Shirley"—also made the rounds of theaters. Astor Pictures had bought up the rights and produced some beautiful theater lobby publicity.

By this time, Mrs. Temple had become so uneasy about Shirley's future at Twentieth Century-

Shirley's scene from Hollywood Steps Out *has her dancing with the very tall Gary Cooper.*

December 30, 1939

PICTUREGOER and FILM WEEKLY

by **WALT DISNEY**

DISNEY IS never more amusing than when he turns his pen loose on the stars. He has done it again in "The Autograph Hound"

In this Autograph Hound *scene, Shirley falls down the steps to sit facing Donald Duck. This illustration is from* British Picturegoer, *December 30, 1939.*

Fox that she began to consider other options. The way Zanuck avoided any direct contact with them personally made her feel that his interest in Shirley was waning. Zanuck's other big stars and films, she believed, had pushed the Temple star to the edge of the Fox galaxy. Yes, *The Blue Bird* was planned, but it had been delayed several times. And with *The Wizard of Oz* in extravagant production elsewhere, what was *Blue Bird's* real future? By the time Zanuck was ready to give the film his full attention—and he planned dramatic sets with attention paid to every minute detail—Mrs. Temple was still unhappy.

The Blue Bird's color schemes required carefully designed makeup so that Shirley would appear at her best in Technicolor, and Zanuck seemed to be expending a great deal of effort and

The boy choir sings on, but it looks like Shirley isn't happy with the note she just hit. Nelson Eddy watched fondly during rehearsal.

money. Just in case the project did not meet expectations, Gertrude had a plan of her own. She went to the Westlake School for Girls to consider it as a possible nonstudio school for Shirley. Attending Westlake would enable her daughter to establish friendships with girls from upper-class homes and obtain a well-rounded education. As a teacher, Miss Klamt had been good—and dear—but surely variety was better. Westlake would place Shirley in a more normal environment.

The Blue Bird was filmed in all its vibrant color, at least partly in answer to *The Wizard of Oz*, and it had a high-class plot and top production efforts. The story was an allegory, teaching a lesson that happiness is found among those we love, not in some distant place. Dorothy returned to Kansas from Oz with a similar lesson, but *The Blue Bird* was much more thoughtful and brainy. Nonetheless, *Oz* was a hit and *The Blue Bird* was considered a bomb. Only much later, as audiences learned to appreciate its quality and message, did the film make a profit.

With *The Blue Bird* finished, Mrs. Temple took

Shirley to Westlake for an interview, which both star and school passed. At midterm, Shirley entered the private school as a seventh grader, making her unable to participate in the blockbuster promotions for *The Blue Bird*. But school proved disappointing. Friendships, enmities, pals, and pariahs had formed before Shirley's arrival, and she found herself relegated to the category of outsider. She lacked many of the graces and disgraces the girls cherished, and studio schooling had not prepared her for classroom performance. The star became the reject.

HOPES FOR *The Blue Bird* were still high when Shirley did another benefit performance. On Christmas Eve 1939 she made her professional radio debut, costarring with Nelson Eddy on CBS's *Screen Guild Theater,* sponsored by Gulf Oil. Performers volunteered or were specifically requested to perform on the program, and the $10,000 fee was paid not to them but to the Motion Picture Relief Fund, which helped movie workers and players who were without savings, jobs, and Social

For purposes of filing this photo of the Westlake pet show, Shirley with her little alligator is crossed off in favor of socialite Peggy Lloyd.

A news photo, actually taken from Young People, *was used to publicize Shirley's departure from the screen. In the film, she is packing her bag to leave show business. On May 13, 1940, it was used to signal her leaving Twentieth Century-Fox.*

The outfit is from down home on the farm, a scene from Young People. *The caption spoke of returning home to her backyard.*

Security. Shirley had a bad cold but appeared anyway, performing scenes from *The Blue Bird*. She listened to Nelson Eddy sing, then joined him in a duet of "Silent Night." Fortunately, there was a boy choir as backup because, having nearly always performed as a soloist, Shirley was not trained to blend her voice with another, especially when that voice was coming from the other side of the stage. Rehearsal was unsatisfying and, Shirley felt, the performance even worse.

When the time came for Shirley to begin filming *Young People*, adjustments were required of both her and Westlake. It soon became clear that Shirley continued to make news. Wherever the star went, the media followed. If she attended a dance at the California Military Institute, cameras singled out her and her partner. Rumors about the Temple-Fox estrangement were spreading, so something as simple as going shopping involved

British TV later summed it up precisely in creating this illustration with the caption: "The best of times—and the worst of times."

facing a barrage of questions, including how it felt to be a washed-up-has-been. Although Shirley was anything but that, how could she possibly respond?

Back at Westlake, Shirley was still unable to find camaraderie. One particular news photo reveals how her status as a person of importance had declined so radically. She had regularly associated with the children of film star Harold Lloyd, who lived nearby. Westlake had its annual pet show with both Shirley and Peggy Lloyd bringing their entries. They posed together, Shirley with her pet alligator and Peggy with a registered spaniel. Surely the alligator would win, even without Shirley! The newspaper, in deciding how to file the photo after use, picked Peggy as the person of interest. Shirley was crossed out, and a notation on the back ordered it to Peggy's file.

Zanuck first planned to follow *Young People* with a film called *Lady Jane*. Usually sure of what he was doing, he seemed uncharacteristically

changeable when it came to Shirley. When the Temples learned that, instead of *Lady Jane*, Shirley's next film would be a two-year-old scenario again revolving around her song-and-dance tricks, they finally acted to end their relationship with the studio. The Temples had at first planned to wait until Shirley's contract expired in 1942 and simply not renew, but the studio's choice of Shirley's next project settled the matter. On April 10, 1940, Mrs. Temple hired Frank Orsatti as Shirley's agent. His job was to get her better pictures, Shirley wrote in *Child Star*, or to get an end to the contract.

Severing the relationship with Twentieth Century-Fox meant that Mrs. Temple would lose her weekly salary of approximately $750 and Shirley would forfeit about $5,000 a week. Brother Jack had only briefly worked at the studio, serving as assistant director on *Pigskin Parade*, with Betty Grable and Judy Garland. By now, he was busy elsewhere with college. Young George was also occupied, having enlisted in the Marines. Mr. Temple would lose his occasional fee as an agent, so there were adjustments for all. The biggest blow came when the studio elected to make a lump sum payment to a special trust fund. The total, reported as $300,000, was considerably less, the bulk of the sum having been privately paid earlier to Shirley's dad.

A British newspaper said it best, though much later, in a graphic created in the 1960s to publicize a nostalgia feature on BBC2 TV that reviewed the war years of 1939 to 1945. The publicity combined a photo of little Shirley atop the outstretched arm of Adolph Hitler giving his "Heil" salute. For the Temple family, for the world, it was as the British caption stated: "The best of times—and the worst of times."

DESPITE HER DEPARTURE from Fox, Shirley was neither retired nor out of the public eye. For another Red Cross benefit, she was visited at the family's Brentwood estate by Gene Autry, and they posed in various locations. Some photos were very serious, and in others Gene was the singing cowboy serenading with voice and guitar. Shirley pretended to be selling him tickets, since the purpose was to persuade people both to buy tickets to the

In this pose, a serious Shirley holds up one of the Red Cross posters. She wears a Red Cross cap, but her outfit is the jumper set worn in Young People. *Cowboy Gene Autry, also looking serious, has his arm around Shirley as an expression of teamwork. On the table beside them is a photo from 1933, when Shirley was a Wampas model.*

Shirley occasionally consented to do publicity that included her friends. When her Campfire group was folding the 1940 Christmas seals for mailing, she permitted this photo to be taken. Some editor missed the boat, incorrectly identifying the seals as for the Red Cross rather than the usual Christmas anti-tuberculosis drive.

Shirley rehearsed the Lux *Captain January* show on January 16. This allowed time to get promos such as this to the media to announce the actual broadcast on January 27.

benefit and to donate to the cause. *Street of Mercy*, broadcast on June 22, 1940, on all three networks, included many star volunteers. Over $250,000 was raised for the Red Cross to provide European war relief.

Journalists of all stripes were busy trying to learn what direction Shirley's career would take next. Richard E. Hays, in his syndicated "Along Film Row" column of August 26, 1940, reported that the Temples would opt for a picture-a-year deal—or a maximum of three pictures in two years. Hal Roach and MGM had made offers, he wrote. Bids by Columbia, Universal, and independent producer Lester Cowan had come in. Hays detailed that Cowan had asked F. Scott Fitzgerald to write *Cosmopolitan* with Shirley in mind. Columbia owned the Gladys Lehman story *June Madness*. Another source reported that a year earlier MGM had bought *Cathleen*, the story of a motherless teen written by Kay Van Riper, coauthor of some of the Hardy family stories. Still, the Temples continued the search for a proper vehicle.

Shirley continued to make radio appearances. On October 14, 1940, she joined Claude Rains for a dramatization of her film *The Littlest Rebel*, although she was a much older Rebel by now and the script had to be rewritten to fit. On January 27, 1941, another of Shirley's films was dramatized on Lux Radio Theater, this time an updated *Captain January*. Her pay per episode was reported to be $5,000, the same amount Fox had been paying for a much more demanding week's work.

America Calling, a charity event staged to benefit Greek War Relief and broadcast from Grauman's Chinese Theatre, aired on NBC in February 1941. Seats sold for $10.00 each, and the participating stars—an impressive array, including Shirley—donated their

Shirley, Myrna Loy, and Tyrone Power chat before the broadcast to raise money for Greece. Shirley is wearing one of the formals designed for her new film, Kathleen.

The stars are interested in young lady Shirley. Among those in the group are Monty Woolley, Melvyn Douglas, and Charles Laughton in back. Those in front include Sam Goldwyn, Clark Gable, Carole Lombard, Myrna Loy, and Tyrone Power.

On a visit to Universal, Shirley met assorted staff and stars. Here, Deanna Durbin, who was making Spring Parade, *gives a gracious welcome.*

Shirley briefly served as an editorial advisor on a children's newspaper, as shown here. Soon, she would advance to the Parents' Institute for a similar position on its new teen magazine, Calling All Girls.

salaries, which would have topped $100,000. The format was similar to that of the modern telethon: in each local area people phoned the NBC affiliate to make donations. A total of $142,000 was raised.

Shirley joined other personalities at the Los Angeles Memorial Coliseum in a benefit for war-damaged Finland. She also made visits to several studios to explore professional possibilities. At Columbia, she met with Rosalind Russell and Rita Hayworth, and at MGM she posed with Mickey Rooney and Judy Garland. This led to rumors that she was being considered for a picture with the latter twosome, perhaps *Babes on Broadway* or *Babes in Hollywood*, a Topsy and Eva story with Judy in blackface. But Mrs. Temple viewed these as supporting roles unbefitting a star. *Panama Hattie* from the stage hit was considered, but it was somewhat vulgar and the role subsequently went to Shirley-imitator Joan Carroll. *Barnacle Bill*, with Wallace Beery, was ruled out as too coarse or common; Virginia Weidler eventually did a great job in the role. *Lucky Sixpence* for Edward Small sounded too much like *Lucky Penny*, the original title of Shirley's film *Just Around the Corner*.

The Temples had very definite preferences. The gifted Joe Pasternak had directed Deanna Durbin and Gloria Jean to great success. Frank Capra at Columbia was another top-ranking and sensitive director they liked. So Shirley paid a visit to Universal. She visited, she posed, she even tried some dance steps. Nothing seemed to click. Rumor had it that she would just do radio or would join Billy Rose's show at the New York World's Fair, which was preparing to open for a second year.

NEW YEAR'S EVE of 1941 was special for the Temple family, for Gertrude and George celebrated their twenty-seventh wedding anniversary, as the press reported, "at the home of Shirley Temple, child film star." At the time this seemed like an outrageous statement, but later revelations support that the Brentwood estate was mostly paid for and maintained using earnings supposedly be-

On January 2, 1941, Shirley signed her first contract with Louis B. Mayer, arranged by longtime Mayer friend and Temple agent Frank Orsatti.

ing held in trust for Shirley. The public already knew that brother George had enlisted in the Marines in 1940 and brother Jack in the U.S. Army Air Force somewhat later. They learned that both brothers announced their engagements at the anniversary party. Mrs. Temple had earlier predicted that both sons would have to elope because Shirley could not be omitted from a formal wedding party, but if included, she would draw attention from the bride. Jack, who was then completing postgraduate work at Stanford, still planned a church wedding and had one of sorts when he and his bride, Miriam, eloped to Las Vegas the following February. George was already somewhere in the Pacific with the Marines.

On January 2, 1941, Shirley signed a contract with Louis B. Mayer at MGM. Everyone had high hopes, but what Mayer offered was not relished by the Temples, and this led to delays. *Cathleen*, now titled *Kathleen*, seemed to be Mayer's choice and wardrobe designing began.

The MGM contract was renegotiated the following April. Shirley wrote of multiple failures as MGM's staff tried to change her entire persona. The new contract specified one film, chosen without Mrs. Temple's approval. That June, *Kathleen* officially began filming. Mrs. Temple would continue to accompany Shirley to the set, and the studio provided reasonable lodging for both, but Gertrude received no salary and had no input. The MGM contract allowed Shirley to make eight yearly radio broadcasts. Her billing would be no less than that of any other star. Given her age, she would still not be required to join the Screen Actors Guild. As required by California law, a judge approved the contract.

Years later, in the May 1946 issue of *Movieland*, an eighteen-year-old Shirley Temple gave advice to budding star Margaret O'Brien in an article penned by Dorothy O'Leary. Although one can't be sure just how much of the advice was coming from Shirley herself and how much from Dorothy, much of it rings true to the way Shirley acted and reacted. In this very revealing article, Shirley cautions Margaret to not measure people by their importance but by their humanity. She advises her not to pry into the affairs of others or to disclose her own. She emphasizes the importance of becoming well-informed, for an actress meets scientists, statesmen, artists, and others with whom she must speak intelligently. Shirley further advises Margaret that she must share the many gifts she receives and regard honors and luxuries as privileges, not as things that are her due. Equally important, Shirley says, is to enjoy oneself.

Although Shirley was nearing the end of her teen years when the *Movieland* article was published, the thoughts expressed seemed to represent the essence of her belief system at that time. She had felt so strongly in her right to privacy that she never admitted that her hair had been bleached or touched up. However, she did speak of the studio having dyed it, perhaps referring to only the teen years. Rather, she wrote of being

unsure what her true hair color was. Shirley was practicing the reticence she advised.

Shirley also did not discuss her age. In 1934, Mrs. Temple had been persuaded by Winfield Sheehan at Fox to accept the studio's "reducing" the age by one year. Of course, Shirley's life insurance policies—Fox took out several—carried the correct date, but otherwise the studio controlled all statements regarding her date of birth. When Shirley celebrated her twelfth birthday and learned from her mom that it was in fact the start of year thirteen, this was both a private and public revelation. The age correction had to be administered from then on because, after all, it had been entered in the *World Book* as 1929, and to everyone that made it a fact.

Throughout Shirley's teen years, reporters' continual attempts to delve into her private life met gentle reserve from both Shirley and her mother. Thus, it was never definitely established that mother and daughter had disagreements or that Mrs. Temple dominated her daughter's life. There were surely times when Gertrude did attempt to control, but these evidently were fewer than rumor led the public to believe, but also more than the "perfect daughter-mother" relationship that publicity implied. In *Child Star*, Shirley shares considerable details of her life at home, deliberately trying to dispel many myths. But the account makes it plain that despite all their foibles, Shirley's family was and is her treasure.

IN THE FALL OF 1941, still finishing *Kathleen*, Shirley was late returning to Westlake. She was now a high-school freshman and a very fashionable one at that, taking all fourteen dresses designed for her in *Kathleen* to augment her school uniform. She also let her hair finally grow out to its natural color of deep brown with reddish highlights. This never ceased to amaze reporters, who seemed to still expect fifty-two blonde baby curls.

At Westlake, Shirley was a follower, not a leader. And at the theaters, *Kathleen* was also a follower—to the main feature. Still, the film and Shirley's work in it was considered solid. Off screen, Shirley was maturing beautifully. She was also showing a decided interest in new things, particularly medicine. At school, she had no objection to dissecting a frog. When her tonsils were removed, she asked many questions and learned the names of the various surgical implements, having agreed to share all the details with her girlfriends. After a local military school party, she came home suddenly aware of various types of class differences. There was so much talk about upper and lower classmen—about lower-uppers and upper-lowers—that she later commented, "Honestly, all I could think of was a pair of false teeth!"

JACK AND MIRIAM TEMPLE had a baby son whom they named John Stanley Temple, Jr., making Shirley an aunt. Oddly, however, she had already become a grandmother. During the United China Relief Fund drive, Shirley had contributed and also signed up to take care of three children, and in China that made her an esteemed grandparent. Talking about that wasn't her style, aside from her little joke of becoming a grandmother before a parent. But she was hardly reticent about her nephew's talents, appearance, all that was wonderful about him. She was also proud, although often worried, about her second serviceman brother, George. Shirley was like any other American girl, writing letters to her siblings and to other servicemen she met at the Hollywood Canteen or at local parties. But she also did some special radio shows for the 1941 Christmas season: four broadcasts in a series called *Shirley Temple Time*. These replaced *Hollywood Première* for the month, with sponsorship by the Elgin Watch Company.

AFTER *KATHLEEN*, SHIRLEY PLAYED a typical teen in *Miss Annie Rooney*. She jitterbugged, though in real life she said she preferred the dreamy dances to being flung about. She got her first screen kiss and coyly refused to discuss any such real-life experience. She spoke in the teen jargon that was popular at Westlake and most other high schools. War had brought military drill to the school, and Shirley worked her way up to the rank of drill sergeant, then lieutenant.

On March 4, 1942, Shirley began her own radio show, *Junior Miss*, which was renewed after the first thirteen weeks. This half-hour CBS series, adapted from the Sally Benson book (and Book-of-the-Month Club selection) of the same title, was sponsored by Ivory Snow. Shirley was featured as "Junior Miss" Judy Graves, no longer a "little miss fix-it," but instead just the opposite. Judy got her family into a weekly scrape involving family, relatives, soldiers, the war effort, scrap drives, contests, and more. Late in 1942, another actress took over for Shirley, presumably because of Shirley's school, film, or other commitments.

DECEMBER 5TH SHOW, costarring Warner Baxter, plus variety show.

DECEMBER 12TH SHOW, *Mr. Ideal,* costarring Robert Young. At the close of this program, Shirley whispered "Hello, George" into the microphone. She was sending greetings to her brother, who had been with the Marines at the Pearl Harbor bombing on December 7. The family had just learned that he was safe and was listening to her broadcasts.

DECEMBER 19TH SHOW, *Christmas for Two,* costarring Lionel Barrymore.

DECEMBER 26TH SHOW, a drama, costarring Humphrey Bogart.

Despite the "Junior Miss" title, earning $3,000 for each weekly dramatization hardly made Shirley a typical young teen. Mary Pickford, of United Artists, bought the film rights to *Junior Miss* and evidently wanted Shirley to film it, but that was not to be, for Peggy Ann Garner eventually got the role. Another period of rejections ensued, with no film, director, or studio contract forthcoming. So, with her career at a standstill, Shirley focused her energies on Westlake, where two new girls had enrolled. Remembering her own rejection, Shirley went out of her way to make Brig and Jane Wilder feel at home. Ironically, in March 1943, David O. Selznick bought the rights to the autobiographical war story written by the Wilders'

(continued on page 95)

On Pearl Harbor day, Shirley graced the cover of the New York Sunday News *magazine, showing the world a lovely young brunette.*

mother, and *Since You Went Away* was on its way to the movie screen.

Meanwhile, Shirley had been corralled by Mary Pickford for a photo announcement proclaiming that Shirley would remake Pickford's *Coquette*. The photo got extremely wide coverage, and although the film idea fizzled, Shirley's potential didn't. Selznick had bought a one-third interest in United Artists, which would release his films. Shirley's youth and potential popularity drew Selznick's attention, and he offered her the role of Brig in *Since You Went Away* with a one-year test contract commencing on April 1, 1943, at $2,200 a week. If all went well, David O. Selznick Productions, Inc., would extend the contract to seven years at $5,000 a week. This was to become Selznick's first film since *Gone With the Wind*.

A New Beginning

Selznick didn't present Shirley as a solo star, but he saw her as a very dear teenager and a team player, and he guided her career carefully. Whether it was the role of Brig or simply the culmination of years of child stardom, servicemen the world over seemed to take Shirley to their hearts. They wrote for photographs, often preferring her to the pinup queens, or sent Shirley pictures of her that they had taken from captured or dead Japanese and German soldiers. Servicemen considered her just the right kid sister or girl-next-door who was young enough to still be single by the time they came home. And when they did, they would crowd the gates at the Temples' North Rockingham estate and Shirley would chat with them and give autographs as she went in and out. The Temples had purchased the Rockingham land—basically a large empty lot—in mid-1936, shortly after they had moved into their second Santa Monica home, at 948 24th Street. They hired an architect to design the estate, in an area now known as Brentwood, and moved in before the pool, stables and riding area, and Shirley's playhouse were built.

Squadron 111 at El Toro Marine Corps Air Station in California was typical of the groups that adopted Shirley as mascot or kid sister. They in-

On March 30, 1942, Shirley made the cover of Life *magazine. That, plus an inside story, featured the glamour photos of Hurrell. This one emphasizes the serious young beauty.*

vited her for a visit and she accepted, sharing chocolate cake and friendly conversation, even trying on a few of the flight jackets. She was a favorite at the Hollywood Canteen, sometimes dancing with a hundred or so fellows in one visit. Her incoming mail was in the thousands, many letters coming from servicemen and marked "free." Her outgoing mail was sizable as well.

During her high-school years, Shirley paid wounded servicemen many hospital visits, but to her this was hardly to be glorified. On the contrary, she was humbled that the visits were treasured and that her fame was able to bring some comfort to those suffering. She listened, visited, sang, and even danced now and then, gladly giving autographs. Mainly, she just tried to say, "I care. Thanks."

Shirley sold $30,000 worth of War Bonds in one afternoon at I. Magnin store in Los Angeles. A Marine guard-of-honor came to celebrate.

Some visits were difficult—one, almost unbearable. Shirley was chatting with a fellow who had lost a leg when suddenly a camerawoman pushed her way to the bedside, pulled off the covers, and announced: "We want a picture of Shirley looking at your leg!" While the young man buried his head in the pillow, Shirley replaced the covers. She no doubt would have liked to make some choice remarks about the woman's cruelty, but she would choose her words carefully. Although Shirley had some colorful vocabulary at her disposal, it would never do for the media to hear her use it and then widely quote her.

Both Temple parents were involved in their daughter's career, school life, and love life. Mother Temple supervised closely, approving and disapproving boys, as she had done with Shirley's pro-

spective film roles. Long-distance phone calls from soldiers were taken by Mr. Temple so that Shirley could focus on her studies, usually to the accompaniment of loud music or the program *Gang Busters*. (She, of course, was glad to answer calls herself.)

The *Since You Went Away* première saw Shirley escorted by Private Andy Hotchkiss, who had been photographed with her at some of the many parties and poolside picnics hosted by various stars, especially Joan Crawford, and Mary Pickford at the Pickfair estate. These were not studio-arranged dates to create photo opportunities. Andy, or "Hotch," a military student and then a serviceman, was her first very serious love.

For the film *I'll Be Seeing You*, Shirley was again guided by Selznick to create a typical kid sister

(Above) More morale-building came with Shirley's appearing before a mass audience of the Cal Ship workers. Admiral Howard Vickery of the U.S. Maritime Commission appeared with her, much more ill-at-ease than she.

(Above right) Shirley made a visit to the Cal Ship yard in California, where some of the lady welders proudly explained their equipment to her.

(Right) Mary Pickford and Shirley share a chat over radio KECA in Hollywood on August 6, 1944. They discussed their recent visits to local military hospitals on this program for the American Red Cross, entitled "Since Pearl Harbor."

For her sixteenth birthday, Shirley showed off the movie dress she had worn in her first big movie hit, Stand Up and Cheer. *The "Baby, Take a Bow" dress, named for her song in the film, was among the Fox costumes bought by Mrs. Temple when she and Shirley left that studio. A little wartime sidelight: notice the sheen of Shirley's rayon hosiery. Nylon had gone to war, especially for parachutes.*

servicemen would come home. The song, which echoed World War I hopes, was just the kind of slow dance tune that Shirley favored. It has continued to be sung and danced to.

With the making of *I'll Be Seeing You*, Shirley's life became hectic. Her trip to New York City in the fall of 1944 is a perfect example. The visit attracted huge attention, and that was followed by a bond tour to Canada. But dates were confusing. News photos dated October 15 showed her arriving from the West Coast, yet according to another news photo date she had visited Forest Hills, New York, on September 4.

Using dated news photos, one can successfully trace Shirley's steps. On August 29 she breezed into New York City and went to the Pennsylvania Station U.S.O. Lounge for an appearance that included serving as a hostess and giving autographs. According to *Redbook*, her visit included several canteen stops, two bond-rally appearances, a trip to the mayor's office (in this case to help Mayor Fiorello LaGuardia stress the importance of waste-paper salvage), plus several rehearsals and radio broadcasts.

The December 1944 issue of *McCall's* told of Shirley taking her mother shopping to select a dress that wasn't black. A news photo dated August 31 showed Shirley selecting a hat at Bonwit Teller; presumably, the hat and dress were purchased during the same excursion. On September 4, Shirley was off to the National Amateur Tennis Championship Tournament at Forest Hills, where she met tennis champ Francisco Pancho Segura, with whom she had made radio broadcasts to various Latin American countries. That same day, she also visited the Central Park Mall for the *New York Daily Mirror* Sports Festival.

image. He gave her extra drama as something of a trouble-causer through a careless slip of the lip. The ramifications of loose talk was a popular theme at the time, even finding its way onto a popular poster proclaiming, "A slip of the lip can sink a ship." In the film, it nearly sank a love affair until apologies and forgiveness brought everyone to a happy ending.

Selznick's newly-formed Vanguard Films released the movie in the summer of 1944. Shirley celebrated her sixteenth birthday on the set that April. *Life* magazine gave the party special coverage, while the film's title song reinforced the happy dream of a time when peace would reign and the

(continued on page 102)

After finishing I'll Be Seeing You, Shirley joined Prime Minister MacKenzie King of Canada to open a war loan drive. She gave nationwide radio speeches in English, and in French when in Montreal. Here she is in Ottawa to launch a ship.

When Shirley visited New York's Pennsylvania Station in the late summer of 1944, she visited with servicemen at the U.S.O. Lounge. The photo is dated August 29.

(Top left) Shirley visited tennis star Francisco Pancho Segura on September 4.

(Top right) Soon after the New York visit, Shirley received an award from Rudy Vallee, broadcast on NBC from Hollywood. Her hair is almost exactly the same as when dancing with Lieutenant Barney Straus.

(Bottom left) The NBC show also featured Fred Allen. Here, holding her award, Shirley checks his script.

(Opposite, top right) At the Central Park Mall, Shirley joined Bill Robinson for a dance demonstration before the Sports Festival crowd.

(Opposite, top left) At the Stork Club, on September 10, Shirley danced with Straus.

(Opposite, bottom) From his regular table at the Stork Club, newsman Walter Winchell kept track of New York City goings-on. On September 6, Shirley was the news. This is an official Stork Club photo.

Shirley christened the Douglas C-54 (C for cargo) airplane at the Santa Monica aircraft plant, reaching to caress her name on its side and wishing it many safe journeys.

There, she met longtime friend Bill Robinson, and they staged a brief dance for the crowd. A photo that made its way back home to the *Examiner* reference library, with receipt dated September 6, showed Shirley dining with Walter Winchell at Sherman Billingsley's Stork Club. Also during the trip, she visited Sardi's and was interviewed by Mel Heimer. On September 10, she had a dance date at the Stork Club with U.S. Army Air Corps Lieutenant Barney Straus. Finally, it was time to go home and rest.

Shirley was honored to be asked to address the *New York Herald-Tribune* forum on October 17. Her topic was, of course, related to motion pictures. She spoke of the need for more films dealing with the psychiatric problems of servicemen.

I'll Be Seeing You had accomplished this in depicting the problems of veteran Joseph Cotten, who experienced flashbacks of war that were sometimes triggered by just the bark of an angry dog. There also was a need for films dealing with those trying to cope with and help veterans returning with physical problems. Society as a whole, especially its youth, needed to be educated.

Shirley also starred for CBS in a *Stage Door Canteen* broadcast with Bert Lytell and then made a radio appearance on *The Johnny Mercer Show*. Following that, accompanied by her parents, she headed north for a personal appearance tour of Canada. Joining Prime Minister MacKenzie King, she made a network radio appeal on behalf of the Seventh War Loan Drive. King later wrote that the crowds were incredible but terrifying—it was Shirley they wanted to see.

In November 1944, Shirley received a very special honor. A C-54 transport plane was named in her honor at the Douglas aircraft plant in Santa Monica, California. The plane held the record on the *Fireball Express* run, taking only six days, ten hours, and fifteen minutes to fly from Miami to India and back. A great deal of cargo was needed to support the India-Burma theater of operations, but naturally the official Air Force news release didn't go into those details. It just publicized Shirley's christening of this particular ship and, of course, made no mention of the B-29, the other great cargo ship made by Boeing. Also, no one even hinted at that old Good Ship Lollipop.

After her first two films under careful Selznick supervision, the remaining five years of Shirley's contract with him were spent in loan-out, that is, "rent-out." He turned down both the stage and film versions of *Cabbages and Kings*, feeling that it wasn't the right piece for her.

Publicity said Shirley was interested in doing stage projects. Publicity also said that Shirley was terrified to appear and perform in public. So much for publicity! Selznick did approve her filming *Kiss and Tell*, over which he had script approval.

The long run of *Kiss and Tell* on Broadway, even after the film rights had been bought for Shirley, gave ample time for critics to analyze the effect such a role would have on her goody-goody (presumed) image. The role called for her to be pregnant out of wedlock, with the storyline boyfriend the alleged father. Much of the action revolved about Shirley's father's hysterical reactions.

Many objected to Shirley doing the film version of *Kiss and Tell*, maintaining that it would spoil her screen and private image, though why is not clear. When filming got underway, Selznick was busy elsewhere, and the writing of F. Hugh Herbert pretty much remained untouched. If Shirley was supposed to be a perfect teen, that was defined more by criticism than by praise.

SHIRLEY MAY HAVE been a role model for many, but her life was anything but ordinary. While filming, she had private on-set tutors so that she could keep current with her Westlake classmates. Her

Shirley posed for the United Nations clothing drive with many of her personal and movie childhood dresses. Here, she holds up the yellow daisy dress from Curly Top, *but the caption attributed it to* Little Miss Marker *and emphasized the new diamond she had received from Sergeant John Agar.*

dress was also not typical. Although she occasionally bought an outfit off the rack, most were designs by Adrian or Jean Louis and others. She never seemed to be homely, awkward, gangly, or the least bit ill-at-ease when reporters asked intrusive, personal questions.

A case in point: The story of *Kiss and Tell* involved Shirley selling kisses to twenty-two servicemen. Counting rehearsals, camera angles, and takes, Shirley gave over one hundred kisses to strangers—many real-life servicemen. Whether just seeking news or gossip, or trying to ferret out a scandal, nervy reporters asked the sixteen-going-on-seventeen-year-old whether she had had any practice. Practice kissing fellows? None of their business! But with great poise, Shirley merely

One of the dozens of engagement photos of Shirley and Jack. Dated April 9, 1945, this one was taken in her home, standing in front of a painting of little child star Shirley.

On May 23, 1945, gunner's mate Christopher Adams met Shirley at her home gate to show a sword taken from a Japanese officer on Okinawa. The caption also stated that Chris had been signed to a postwar movie contract by David O. Selznick in 1943 and would return after the war for leading man roles opposite Shirley.

replied, "Of course not." Then she pointed out that a guy who received a kiss in the film was promoted from extra to bit player, and his pay doubled as a result.

Shirley exhibited more typical teenage behavior when she began to learn to drive a girlfriend's car without first securing a driving permit. When her parents found out, they stopped her, explaining that if anything happened it would make news all over the country. Of course, they were also concerned about her safety. And they were at least as concerned for the safety of the many who would copy her carelessness or use her as an excuse for their own disobedient behavior. Shirley had said that films should have a positive influence. She had even told the *Herald-Tribune* forum that youth shouldn't see films about delinquency, which would serve to promote bad ideas. Likewise, the Temples advised Shirley, she better not be a negative influence on other youngsters through her conduct in real life.

As for good ideas, there seemed to be no shortage of ways in which people wanted to use Shirley to promote their respective causes. Studio hangers-on and members of society were not reluctant to suggest (subtly or in the form of veiled threats) how she should help and thus encourage others to contribute. Ladies of the UNRRA (United Nations Relief and Rehabilitation Administration) clothing drive came to Shirley asking for garments and soliciting help in getting others to contribute items for refugees and the war-ravaged. They knew that Mrs. Temple had saved Shirley's movie costumes, and they let it be known that Shirley ought to set an example by acting charitably. There was no assurance that the costumes would actually ever be sent overseas.

Good items in many drives tended to be "diverted" by the workers, and this certainly would have been true of *any* Shirley dress, from a movie or not. Still, Shirley retrieved some of the dresses from storage and posed with them—including a print pinafore she wore during the filming of *The Poor Little Rich Girl* and a dark print bolero dress from *Little Miss Broadway*. Publicity implied that Shirley had donated the costumes to UNRRA, although a news byte explained that Gertrude decided to keep some in case Shirley ever had a daughter. One photo caption—either crassly or accurately—suggested that the occasion gave Shirley a chance to show off her engagement ring.

In *Child Star*, Shirley writes of a great many romances and quite a few semi-engagements. Westlake classmate Joyce Agar had a tall soldier brother named John (Jack), who turned up at a few of the get-togethers. During *I'll Be Seeing You*, Shirley and Jack began to date, and by *Kiss and Tell* it was a serious romance, though not exclusive according to Shirley's narrative. Not yet. More like, as some girls felt, one more scalp added to the trophy belt. She wrote of still being tentative when she accepted the gorgeous diamond solitaire engagement ring.

By the time *Kiss and Tell* was in general release, Shirley had graduated from Westlake in a long lace frock. Nevertheless, for its May 1945 cover, *Screen Guide* insisted on a white cap and gown for the graduate. At her senior luncheon, Shirley wasn't trying very hard to hide the great diamond ring

(Top right) Shirley's June 15 graduation from Westlake School for Girls featured formal lace gowns chosen by the girls. The dresses of all graduates were the same, but few of the girls looked as lovely as Shirley.

(Bottom right) Here is a special glamour pose for Kiss and Tell, *proclaiming a grown-up young lady.*

Shirley and Jack are flanked in the receiving line by mother Gertrude Temple and matron of honor Miriam Temple, wife of Shirley's brother Jack, who was best man.

Amid onlookers, Shirley begins to cut the wedding cake at the reception held at the family's Brentwood home.

that pledged her troth to Sergeant Agar. All over America, thinking of Shirley's impending marriage made people feel older. Shirley's contemporaries, on the other hand, felt themselves maturing right along with her.

Segeant Jack had endeared himself to Gertrude Temple. The engagement had strong parental approval, on condition that the marriage would not take place for several years. Shirley wanted to be the first in the Westlake class to become engaged—and she was. She turned seventeen in April of 1945. She agreed to delay the marriage, but young love and war uncertainties changed that along with her discovery that Gertrude had married at seventeen. Her mom confessed that she had also wanted to be the youngest in her class to marry, so she had reduced her age by two years. But through her admission Gertrude had lost her trump card, plus the sergeant wanted a wife before going overseas.

Anticipating that Jack might be sent out of the country on short notice, he and Shirley decided to set a wedding date of September 19, coinciding with the start of a fifteen-day pass. The Temples gave their approval, and a traditional church wedding was planned. In the end David Selznick chose a larger church, staged the wedding, and paid for it. Seventeen-year-old Shirley was attended by stand-in Mary Lou Isleib and some of her Westlake girlfriends. While rehearsing before the ceremony, she was told that a crowd of some ten thousand fans was waiting outside. Her quixotic reply? "I must be slipping. Jeanette MacDonald had twenty thousand."

Rather than fill the church with stars, Shirley chose to invite friends, including prop men, scrubwomen, all the real people who had helped her and whom she treasured. The wedding was no flashy affair—fairy tale perhaps . . . and dreamy . . . and certainly the wedding of Selznick's "ideal" star. But still, the focus was on a very tender-eyed young girl in love with love. Producers noted the tall good-looking groom, and soon they were inquiring as to his acting status. Certainly, they were not unaware of the publicity value he had attained as Shirley's husband.

Contrary to expectations, rather than being shipped overseas, Jack returned to camp at

In her Howard Greer gown, bride Shirley looks adoringly at new husband John Agar in his Uncle Sam suit. The date was September 19, 1945.

Geiger Field. During the next four months, he shuttled between assorted bases on the West Coast, possibly as a physical education instructor. Discharged from the U.S. Army Air Corps in February 1946, Jack was on hand to help celebrate Shirley's eighteenth birthday on the *Honeymoon* set.

For the film, she got another wedding gown and posed for endorsements of everything from silverware to cedar chests. She was featured on the covers of movie magazines with great frequency, while articles presented her advice and opinions on marriage as though suddenly she had become an expert.

The Bachelor and the Bobby Soxer gave Shirley a return to teenage status and comedy. It still ranks as a top picture, partly because of Cary Grant and

Rudy Vallee. Meanwhile, husband Jack was in the process of returning to civilian life, posing for lots of photos at events with his new wife and setting up housekeeping on the Brentwood estate in a remodeled playhouse of no small dimensions. Complete with soda fountain, doll displays, and a theater, Shirley's spacious ten-room home had been stylishly redecorated by Mrs. Temple with modern furnishings. The newlyweds' house was the subject of numerous photo studies, and Shirley and Jack were invariably shown as happy lovebirds.

THAT HAGEN GIRL, in which Shirley appeared with Ronald Reagan in 1947, had overtones of tragedy. Shirley played the title character, who was gossiped about as illegitimate and finally attempted suicide. Later, Shirley was quoted as saying that she wanted to play a really bad girl, but Mary Hagen was just too sad. Fans loved her beautiful performance as Juliet in the "play within the film," though no one paid much attention to Romeo. But then, fans simply loved Shirley—anytime, anywhere.

On January 7, 1947, Shirley made an appearance on Bob Hope's radio show. On March 13, she presented the Academy Award to Claude Jarman, Jr., and to Harold Russell for his role in *The Best Years of Our Lives*. Jack watched as the newest child star got his Oscar, but the outstanding performance to be honored was that of Russell, a returned veteran who was minus both arms and who used prosthetic pincer fingers.

Shirley's next film, *Fort Apache*, was notable and loved because her costar was husband Jack Agar. This seemed like natural progress in togetherness. Shirley and Jack made other films, both together

(Top) Scads of poses like this one depicted the seemingly idyllic marriage of the Agars. They often accompanied features in which Shirley gave advice to other newlyweds.

(Bottom) Linda Susan's arrival meant many features on proper baby care to accompany lots of baby and happy-couple poses. But this photo, dated October 13, 1949, instead broke the news of the marital split.

and apart, and Shirley's fan-club journals, titled *Shirley Scoops*, carried all the news—including snaps of Shirley idolizing Jack, which she truly did. Rumors of impending motherhood began and confirmation was not far behind. Next came a great blast of publicity and pictures of young mother Shirley and her naturally beautiful baby girl, Linda Susan, who came into the world on January 30, 1948. Fans bought the magazines, often two copies of each to save both sides in their scrapbooks. But film roles seemed to diminish in importance and quality, even while fans remained loyal.

Loyalty to Shirley was so strong that when news of a divorce exploded on October 13, 1949, she received some thirty thousand letters, 85 percent sympathetic. As Shirley later

Shirley and Charles Alden Black in Washington, D. C. He was recalled to duty in April 1951, and they drove from California to Washington, stopping off in Oklahoma for an emergency appendectomy for Shirley.

wrote in *Motion Picture* magazine, "My first marriage was a mistake. I am not afraid to think about it or to remember it, but I would rather not discuss it. It was no one's fault. It just should never have happened."

Even a life that seemed as specially endowed as Shirley's had its share of pain. Her breakup affected a great many people, hurting some, shocking others, and drawing criticism from still others, especially columnists who thrived on Hollywood gossip. They fought to claim who knew it first, who saw it coming, or who nobly kept silent. Perhaps the hardest part for Shirley was making her innermost feelings public. Nonetheless, with the publication of her autobiography in 1988 Shirley felt liberated.

One thing was very right about Shirley's marriage to Jack, and that was Susan, as Linda Susan came to be called. Shirley was concerned about her daughter's well-being, and after the divorce was final in 1950, Susan and Shirley were to find a safe haven in Charles Alden Black.

Shirley met Charles while vacationing in Hawaii with her parents and Susan a few months after filing for divorce. A decorated World War II Navy veteran, he was a highly eligible young man according to the various people who gave parties for Shirley in Hawaii. Charles was interested in the environment, the sea, but not films or stars. Then, suddenly, he was interested in Shirley and her little girl. Shirley and Charles were married in a private ceremony on December 16, 1950, and he eagerly adopted Susan.

John Agar continued in films, sometimes staying with his mother in Beverly Hills, making headlines almost as much for drunk driving as for film success. He ceased to be a part of the life of both Shirley and Susan.

The new family had barely settled down in California when Charles was recalled to Navy duty and assigned to Washington, D.C. Shirley accompanied him and led a happy private life as a housewife and mother. When baby Charlie arrived at the Navy hospital on April 28, 1952, he was fine,

This portrait of Shirley was the initial publicity done for her Storybook.

theatrical role. Singling out Susan while ignoring the other children led to Shirley's removing her daughter from both the production and the school. *Time* and *Newsweek* picked up the story. The media didn't understand that publicity was like a school bully, ruining it for everyone. The only actual publicity Shirley willingly accepted during this time was for her doll collection, left behind on loan to a Los Angeles museum.

Movieland of May 1953 reported the Black family's prospective return to California, saying that Shirley had sold her California home, the remodeled playhouse, before going east. Other news had her resting at the home of her parents once the family arrived west. Susan later pointed out two new indentations in Shirley's face, explaining that she got them after a bout with chicken pox. During that illness, Shirley's father helped with the house-hunting. On April 9, 1954, shortly after they settled into a new home in Atherton, daughter Lori was born. Caring for home and family was plenty for young mother Shirley to handle.

As Susan, Charlie, and Lori grew older and required less attention, Shirley branched out into community affairs. She began multiple sclerosis volunteer work in 1954; in 1955, the Peninsula Children's Theater Association was added; in 1956, she did volunteer work at the Stanford Children's Convalescent Hospital Auxiliary; in 1958, much time was given to the Mid-Peninsula Children's Health Council. Little by little, Shirley Temple enlarged her scope to include not only the theater she knew since childhood but also an interest in health and medicine, fields she considered vitally important. The runway has led from there to the world.

Bringing the Magic to Television

Shirley was lured back into show business in January 1957 with *The Shirley Temple Storybook*, a midseason television presentation that dramatized well-known children's stories. Although reminiscent of some of the early Shirley Temple films, the programs had less music and dance, the characters were mostly adult, and the only recurring star was hostess Shirley herself. She introduced and nar-

but due to inept care Shirley nearly died. Publicity again engulfed her. What had been planned to widely publicize the quality of medical care in the Navy instead proclaimed exactly the opposite, particularly the incompetence of egocentric officers and top brass.

In Washington, D.C., Shirley and Charles, accompanied by daughter Susan, paid a visit to President Dwight David Eisenhower at the White House, just as Shirley had visited Mrs. Truman there earlier. There was the occasional Navy and embassy affair, but for the Blacks it was mostly a quiet life. In the fall of 1952, Susan enrolled in kindergarten, and that Christmas she participated with the rest of her class in the kindergarten pantomime. It was an occasion for all students and parents to savor, but somehow newspapers were alerted and proclaimed Susan the star in her first

First publicity for one of Shirley's gowns shows her being fitted by Maria Johnson. Also shown are a screen, fancy furniture, and another gown for the show.

Beauty (Claire Bloom) and the Beast (Charlton Heston) look at an old storybook and confer with hostess Shirley Temple.

rated each story and sang the theme song, "Dreams Are Made for Children." Among the things about which children could dream were the sumptuous gowns worn by Shirley. As she spoke and sang, Shirley looked straight into the camera right where her own children's eyes would be focused.

The resumption of Shirley's career had been a topic of much discussion within the Black family. Shirley herself was concerned that going back to work would mean spending much time, including some overnight, away from home. To minimize the separation, she decided to commute to work from the Black home in Woodside, California.

"A DREAM IS A FAIRY TALE," Shirley sang, and most of the stories dramatized on *The Shirley Temple Storybook* were in fact just that. The series began with a very elaborate staging of *Beauty and the Beast*, starring Claire Bloom as Beauty and Charlton Heston as the Beast.

Judging from the publicity generated, *The Shirley Temple Storybook* was an immediate success, not because NBC worked overtime on promotion, but because Shirley was news and this carried over to her professional involvement. *Redbook* gave Shirley a cover and inside story in January of 1957. *Life* had to wait until February 3, but both the cover and inside color spread were special; the magazine explained that the show would present sixteen stories by the following December. In March, *Children's Playmate* featured Shirley and her children on the cover.

Storybook featured top stars in each episode, even those in which Shirley herself appeared. Although many loved everything about the show, some faulted Shirley's acting. Nonetheless, the bulk of the criticism was that the stage settings, all done in the studio, resembled those of the average high-school play. Television was not yet up to the much-needed location shooting and special effects that give fairy tales a realistic base.

By the time *Storybook* was on the air, the distributor/syndicate NTA had assembled a series of early Shirley films and marketed them on television. They were hugely successful, inspiring a whole new generation of enthusiastic fans. One sponsor was Ideal, maker of the new Shirley Temple doll in sturdy vinyl plastic. When Shirley's first daughter, Linda Susan, was born, Ideal had sought but been denied permission to create a doll of the baby, or even mother-daughter dolls. Shirley cooperated fully.

Shirley was also involved in Saalfield's issuing new paper dolls and coloring books with Shirley's likeness, in Western's issuing more Shirley tablets, and in Cinderella's manufacturing a full line of Shirley dresses for little girls. She even included daughter Lori in some of the dress promotion.

Around this same time, Random House published storybooks of Shirley's films and fairy tale collections using the *Storybook* name.

In a typical opening, the hostess sang amid drapery and chandeliers as she gently glided towards the camera.

Shirley had long ago learned how publicity could be used to advantage, and she made herself readily available for personal appearances and autograph sessions. All of her efforts helped attract a television audience.

Even with all the attendant publicity, *The Shirley Temple Storybook* was in need of help. Each episode was presented as a special shown in no regular time slot, so it was impossible for the show to build up a following. Newspaper television listings helped, but many people didn't consult them

and therefore had no way of knowing when the next *Storybook* would be aired.

Erratic scheduling and poor story adaptations ultimately spelled the show's downfall. Still, *The Shirley Temple Storybook* was important enough to warrant it and its star being featured in at least fourteen TV and magazine sections. Editors always had plenty of fodder from which to choose, but they obviously favored Shirley. The show led to her leading the 1959 Macy's Thanksgiving Day Parade, with Susan marching alongside carrying a version of the

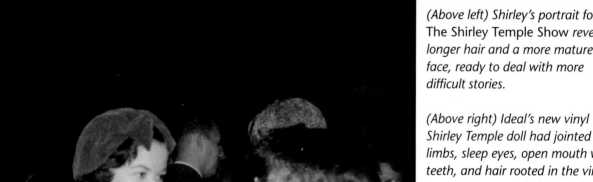

(Above left) Shirley's portrait for
The Shirley Temple Show *reveals
longer hair and a more mature
face, ready to deal with more
difficult stories.*

*(Above right) Ideal's new vinyl
Shirley Temple doll had jointed
limbs, sleep eyes, open mouth with
teeth, and hair rooted in the vinyl.
It came in assorted sizes, as Shirley
shows here. Some even came with
Storybook costumes.*

*Shirley, wearing a grey suit and
yellow-green velvet hat, is
autographing the Random House
Shirley Temple Storybook at a
downtown Los Angeles store.*

The Christmas 1958 Storybook *was a Mother Goose show in which Shirley played Polly Baker to Elsa Lanchester's Mother Goose. That's Charlie, with short jacket and dark hair, on the left. For his role, which involved climbing on a pole to watch for the prince and announce his arrival, he received $590. Daughters Susan and Lori were silent players, together receiving $800.*

new thirty-six-inch Shirley doll. It also led to Shirley's opening a castle at Disneyland.

SHIRLEY'S SECOND SERIES, *The Shirley Temple Show*, which attempted to bring both old favorites and lesser-known stories by beloved writers to the television screen, debuted on September 18, 1960. In the première episode, "The Land of Oz," Shirley played both Princess Ozma and a small boy named Tip. Jonathan Winters, Sterling Holloway, Arthur Treacher, and the always fabulous Agnes Moorehead supported temporary princess Shirley. Most viewers expected *The Wizard of Oz* and were baffled by the differences, failing to recognize a different Oz book.

In a subsequent episode, a fun musical entitled "The Reluctant Dragon," Shirley was something of a princess again, but she had more chance for drama in "The Terrible Clock-man" and "Onawandah," a story by Louisa May Alcott, best known for her book *Little Women*. But *The Little Mermaid*, adapted from Hans Christian Andersen, and MacDonald's *The Princess and the Goblins* both lacked in plot and staging. Everybody tried very hard, but the stories simply were changelings.

The hour-long *Shirley Temple Show* was broadcast in full color each Sunday evening on NBC. It had the advantage of a regular time slot and was a lead-in for the new *National Velvet* series, but at midseason it faced the popular *Maverick* show, in

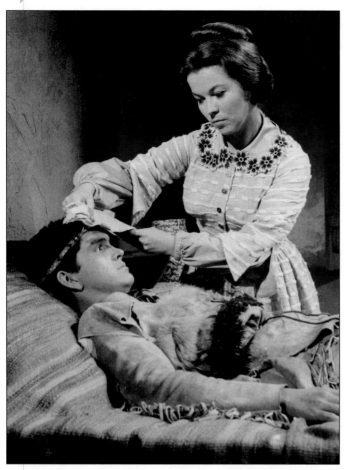

In the story "Onawandah," Shirley is Widow Winters, shown caring for a sick Indian boy, played by David Kent. The hour-long color episode, with its Native American connection, was considered so important that it received first-run publicity when it aired in repeat on July 23, 1961.

its fourth season on another network. Shortly thereafter, additional competition came from Walt Disney, which also had a reputation for drastically adapting stories. Ultimately, it was the ratings race that led to the unfortunate demise of *The Shirley Temple Show*.

In the 1950s and 1960s—in addition to appearing in numerous clips shown as part of television tributes to the Oscars, Twentieth Century-Fox, Darryl F. Zanuck, and the like—Shirley made occasional TV guest appearances. She joined Art Carney and Janis Paige for a Chevy special and sang and danced on *The Dinah Shore Show* on May 4, 1958. A planned 1960 appearance with Dinah was cancelled due to a scheduling conflict. On

February 3, 1964, and again in an August 3 rerun, Shirley joined Mitch Miller to sing along with Leslie Uggams and the Gang. Their "Hello, Shirley" adaptation of "Hello, Dolly" pretty well summed up their feelings and those of other fans.

Shirley celebrated her thirty-fifth birthday while filming Red Skelton's opener for the fall 1963 season. That made the papers along with confusing announcements that she would appear on the show on April 20. Viewers had to wait until September 24 to see bride Shirley as a stylistic foil to Red's beloved tramp. Then she turned hobo and sported a dirty face for one of the rarest moments in her show-business career.

In June of 1964, Shirley hosted a special entitled *Shirley Temple Presents Young America on Stage*, broadcast on KGO-TV in San Francisco. Aimed at the problems of juveniles, the two-hour show featured a few ex-Mousketeers and many amateurs promoting the importance of education and encouraging kids to make the most of opportunities. But Shirley also participated in small-town affairs. She served as the queen of the Palm Springs Twenty-third Annual Circus Days, as she had in childhood and teen years. The year 1967 saw her participate in the Redwood City Centennial celebration in May, and then serve as Grand Marshal of the Fourth of July parade.

Shirley's various social and charitable activities, including her Junior League work, frequently made the news. For the 1963 benefit première of *It's a Mad, Mad, Mad World* for the San Francisco Press Club's scholarship fund, she even posed being arrested by two Keystone Cops. In June 1963, she helped with the KQED auction to raise funds for San Francisco's educational television channel. She began by selling a five-foot-long boa constrictor for $65.00. In 1964, she auctioned off a mink coat.

Shirley's activities continued to be many and varied. She and husband Charles joined John Raitt for a pre-*Carousel* dinner, and made news when she shook her fist at novelist Niven Busch for his parody of California politicians. She recorded a cassette tour for the U.S. museum and art gallery celebrity series of guided lectures, and she donated wood carvings for a charity auction. In 1964, she received a special award for her contributions to Bay area educational television, and even per-

(continued on page 119)

Shirley Temple & Family

This view of the Black family was used on tablet and scrapbook covers.

Shirley and her children were photographed to publicize the Christmas Day 1960 *Shirley Temple Show* episode, *"Babes in Toyland."*

Shirley shows ex-Mouseketeer Annette Funicello her miniature Oscar from 1935. It is 1961, at an Oscar event, and Shirley is wearing an electric *blue gown, the same adjective used to describe the Shirley Temple blue gowns worn by her attendants when she married John Agar.*

formed for Junior League as a mermaid in a million dollars' worth of jewelry—not her own. In November of that year, Shirley was given another award, this time from the California State Teachers' Association for outstanding service to the youth community and schools.

In 1965, Shirley Temple Black was on the board of the Ninth Annual San Francisco International Film Festival. She made an appearance along with Walt Disney, Bing Crosby, a lineup of notable directors, their films, and her own film *The Bluebird*. It was quite a momentous affair. In 1966, Shirley was again on the festival board, but this time she protested the inclusion of the film *Night Games*, which she characterized as "pornography for profit." She didn't posture or pout as some accounts charged, nor did she predict box-office failure. She simply didn't want to be associated with any organization that seemed to recommend the film. Actually, Shirley wasn't the first to criticize *Night Games*; some adults at the Venice Film Festival had sharply attacked it.

Shirley's reaction to the film was used to promote it in San Francisco and other cities from Los Angeles to Anchorage. In Toronto, Patrick Scott wrote, "This may well have been the most commendable performance Miss Temple has ever given. It's not so much that *Night Games* is dirty, it's just that it's so slimy—and also so dull."

Shirley explained her position on *Night Games* and related matters in a centerfold feature entitled "Sex at the Box Office," which appeared in the January 1967 issue of *McCall's* magazine. *Esquire* took a while to formulate its ideas, and in its August 1968 issue it blasted Shirley for her stand on the film and her comments on surgery (she said she enjoyed watching operations) and magazines that showed medical illustrations. "The Gutsmut Game," *Esquire* called it, and although there might have been some truth to the charge that the illustrations in question were feeding the thirst of some for violence, the magazine's real intention was to attack Shirley and her stand on decency.

Giving Hope to Others

In 1952, Shirley's brother George had been diagnosed with the nerve disorder multiple sclerosis, which meant that his life in sports would soon be over, followed by the inability to even care for himself. At the time, there was no hope for remission; the sole certainty was that an MS victim would face a gradual but continual decline. In response to her brother's unfortunate fate, Shirley became very active in the fight to conquer the dreaded disease. She worked for the KNXT Multiple Sclerosis Give-a-Thon in 1954, of which Mickey Rooney was master of ceremonies. In 1960, she accepted for the first time the national chairmanship of their Hope Chest Fund campaign, and in 1963, as part of the *San Francisco Examiner's* "Encounter" series, she discussed the disease with neurologist Knox Finley. This was all part of her continuing desire to acquaint others with problems related to the disease and the efforts being made to find a cure.

When the National Multiple Sclerosis Society celebrated its fifth anniversary with a fashion show at the Sheraton-Park Hotel in Washington, D. C., Shirley served as honorary chairman while Mrs. Richard Nixon was a gracious patron. For some unexplained reason, pictures of the event, dated March 19, 1959, show Shirley with Mamie Eisenhower. Around this time, there were hints that Shirley might soon be involved in government, possibly with the Department of Health, Education and Welfare. Concerned that it might be considered demeaning to the adult Shirley, a "Lollipop" routine that was scheduled to be performed at the event was cancelled. While in Washington, she presented the MS Bronze Hope Chest Award to Don Hearn of the *Washington News*.

In May 1959, Shirley was back in the nation's capital to copresent President Richard Nixon an award marking the start of a five-year program to raise ten million dollars for MS research. She took home Nixon's autograph for her father, who was then celebrating his eighty-first birthday. It was something of a switch for the star to be seeking an autograph, though as a youngster Shirley had amassed a veritable sheaf of autographs of performers and world leaders. As for Shirley's own signature, some newspapers commented that hers was worth twelve of someone else, one reporting that a mail-order firm offered a Temple autograph for $4.50 and that of former President Harry Truman for $2.50.

In the spring of 1964, ABC and Twentieth Century-Fox approached Shirley about starring in another show for television. Script ideas were developed, and by the following January Shirley began preparations for *Go Fight City Hall!*, a half-hour situation comedy in which she would play a single social worker at a San Francisco welfare agency. Singer Bill Hayes was to be her boyfriend, and Temple imitator Victoria Meyerink, from *The Danny Kaye Show*, would be her daughter. One of the little bits of gossip surrounding the proposed sitcom was that the Black family objected to Shirley's dyeing her hair blonde for the role. Eventually it was decided that she would wear a red wispy wig. Color of her hair aside, the pilot didn't sell. Another proposed series, *The Shirley Temple Show* (no relation to the 1960 show with the same name), was to be written by James Komack and coproduced by Cluny Productions and Fox. It would send Shirley, her farming expert husband, and their children into a situation combining *The Egg and I* with *Green Acres* in a setting beyond backwoods. Fortunately, it didn't even achieve pilot status.

March 14, 1965 saw Shirley and Charles, now Ampex vice-president, arrive in London for a six-day stopover visit. Wire services carried pictures from the start of the trip at San Francisco International Airport until its conclusion three weeks later. Notable was a London *Daily Mirror* feature by Shirley, "My Mission to Moscow," in which Charles was quoted considerably.

On March 19, the Blacks arrived in Russia, the chief purpose of the visit being to confer with Soviet doctors, particularly a Dr. Zilver, regarding that nation's progress against multiple sclerosis. But there was also time for sightseeing. At the GUM department store, not far from their hotel at the entrance to Red Square, Shirley bought a beige mink hat and some gifts. The puppet theater pleased her with printed English translations. Other highlights were a visit to a Moscow film theater, seeing the cosmonauts welcomed home in Red Square, and taping a brief television speech. But Shirley was very disappointed on March 25 when she was denied a visit to former premier Nikita Khrushchev, who had invited her when he was in Hollywood in 1959.

Shirley accomplished her purpose in meeting with Dr. Zilver, but found she had more information to share than he. "I am one of those persons who feels that any personal contact can't but help," she said. Later, she used personal interaction to advantage after a Russian made a derogatory statement about the United States: she refused to exchange toasts until he apologized. As it had in London, Russian television used the occasion of Shirley's visit to rebroadcast some of her old movies and clips—and again they were popular.

There was one sad footnote to the Moscow visit. Back home in San Francisco, Charles's father died at the age of eighty-four. His had been a full life, but that didn't lessen Charles's regret at not being there to say a last goodbye or again express his love. The tour ended in Holland with pleasant views of the National Flower Exhibit surrounding Shirley.

In September 1965, Shirley again headed overseas, this time with eleven-year-old Lori. Mother and daughter went to Vienna to attend a medical conference and gain further information on multiple sclerosis that would help Shirley achieve the goal of setting up an international organization for sharing research and information on the disease. Photographers caught Shirley and Lori sightseeing, en route to the Paris airport, and then during a London stopover. Lori went Beatle-hunting while Shirley addressed an MS conference at the Savoy Hotel. London's *Weekend* reporter was all dewy-eyed to report that Shirley's purpose in visiting Vienna was not to partake of that city's legendary pleasures, but to seek information that would help others. French, Italian, even New Zealand media reported the news.

Few papers had carried the local Atherton, California, story that just before her trip Shirley had completed an MS fundraising tour or that Charles had been named to the advisory board of the University of Santa Clara's School of Business. He was also just beginning a new project that would later involve undersea research.

Entering Government Service

By mid-August 1967, it was decided that Shirley would run for the United States Congress in San

Mateo County, California, to fill the position vacated by the late Representative J. Arthur Younger. In July, Governor Ronald Reagan appointed her as public representative on the Advisory Hospital Council and Charles to the Governor's Task Force. Shirley and Charles had both been active in Republican politics long before, with Shirley being swamped for autographs at the 1964 Republican National Convention in San Francisco. Shirley's congressional campaign made headlines worldwide. Canada kept up regular reports in English and French. Great Britain, France, Spain, Italy, even Russia covered it on a continuous basis.

Newspaper morgues were well supplied with photographs of the child Shirley, and nearly every movie role was pictured during the congressional campaign. Film clips were aired repeatedly. *Time*, *Life*, and *Look*, as well as most of the big Sunday newspaper magazine sections, ran features on the candidate, with the publicity strongly divided between ridicule of Shirley and of the professional politicians she was trying to join, suggesting that a shining star was as good in Congress as a bunch of hams. Many genuinely supported Shirley's conservative views. Others, fans of former days, found that—for a while at least—Shirley was again available for letters and autographs by mail or in person. Donations poured in from all over the United States, and Shirley pins, picture slogan cards, and other campaign memorabilia were treasured.

Shirley's family was squarely behind her candidacy, and she herself led a very active hands-on campaign, knocking on doors and meeting people at every opportunity. Although some of the Temple-for-Congress rallies were heavy with song-and-dance routines, much like national conventions, the candidate tried to keep her activities dignified. Bing Crosby hosted a $100-a-plate fundraising dinner and gave staunch support. Governor Reagan, Senator George Murphy of California, former president Dwight D. Eisenhower, and many others showered her with approval; still others despised her.

Whereas the United States said that Shirley was running for office, British papers reported that she was "standing" for office, and New Zealanders called it "sitting" for office. Whatever it was, running for office made her a ready target for car-

I will appreciate your support November 14th.
Shirley Temple Black

Shirley Temple Black

Contributors by mail to Shirley's 1967 congressional campaign received a thank you in the form of this card. The back carried statements of her policies on various issues.

toons, television spoofs, and the hate jibes of columnists. When Shirley lost the general election on November 15, world headlines were not that Pete McCloskey had won but that Shirley had lost. It was likely quite galling for the victor to come in second even in victory.

Rodney G. Minott wrote a book for his friend Pete called *The Sinking of the Lollipop*, which told the story of how Shirley had been defeated. There was irony even in that, for many of the book's buyers were Shirley fans who purchased it only because it was about the woman they loved.

In capitulation, Shirley—some said glowing as though she had won—promised to return to poli-

Shirley makes one of many 1968 appearances on behalf of MS. The National Multiple Sclerosis Association furnished a group of these photos to members of the Shirley Temple Collectors Club that honors her birthday each year with an auction to raise funds for the association.

Hollywood, it parodied Shirley and some of her costars. Bayn Johnson played Shirley, with a gentler Robbi Morgan as replacement. Local productions, a cast album, and even a boxed paper doll followed.

Shirley had entered politics out of a desire to improve things, and in election year 1968 she volunteered to be part of the speakers' bureau of the Republican National Party. From January to November, she campaigned in twenty-one states, forty-six cities, and five foreign countries. In April, she visited various locations in Illinois, then returned to San Francisco with the defensive but true comment, "If you are not involved, the alternative is corrosive apathy."

In May, Shirley spoke at the Honolulu Press Club luncheon, then her speaking took her to Seattle and Tacoma, to Anchorage and Fairbanks, and then on to Texas, where a man squeezed her hand so hard he bruised the ligaments. From there, it was on to Illinois and Ohio. Being squeezed was particularly bothersome to Shirley, for she sometimes came home black-and-blue. A Shirley fan wrote proudly of attending a speech and pressing Shirley's arm gently as she moved down the aisle to the front. It was such a thrill to the fan, but to Shirley it must have felt like one more attack on her person. Other fans dragged out Shirley Temple dolls to be autographed. Less annoying were the cameras and tape recorders.

In August of 1968, in her capacity as cofounder and vice-president of the International Federation of Multiple Sclerosis Societies, Shirley headed for Czechoslovakia. After her arrival on August 18, she posed prettily in the rain. Her purpose in Czechoslovakia was clear: to negotiate that country's joining of the federation. She met with the minister of health who, to Shirley's pleasure and in keeping

tics. Photographs of the moment show Shirley backed by her entire family, but it was the beautifully tragic face of daughter Susan that seemed to stand out.

Even after her unsuccessful bid for elective office, Shirley continued to be a desirable subject for cartoons and satirists. In 1967, *Curley McDimple*, a stage show with music and lyrics by Robert Dahdah, based on a book by him and Mary Boylan, opened in New York. Claiming to be about 1930s with a more liberal government policy, granted his approval.

While in Czechoslovakia, Shirley greatly enjoyed a visit and discussion with a group of neurologists and biochemists at Prague's Charles University. She also enjoyed making contact with the ordinary people, for she was aware that it was they who had made her popular. Nice as she tried to be, however, assertiveness was sometimes in order. For example, at an official luncheon she requested a glass of cold milk. But she was advised, possibly with some indulgence, that the current fad was hot milk with Slivovic, the plum brandy. She simply loved the milk, but cold and without alcohol. Mrs. Black insisted and prevailed.

On the day of her scheduled departure for Copenhagen, Shirley was awakened by hotel staff announcing, "We have been invaded!" In an account published in the January 1967 issue of *McCall's*, Shirley detailed the long wait in the hotel, mostly cut off from local and overseas contacts while Russian tanks moved back and forth throughout the city. She revealed how many Czech friends slipped quietly into the hotel to see how she was doing, and how an increasing number of strangers, some in uniform, also began to move among the waiting people, even setting up checkpoint tables in some hallways. One lady came asserting that Shirley's safe escape was all arranged, but she must come immediately. Still, Shirley insisted that she could not leave behind scores of her fellow Americans, business people and tourists, nor could she disobey American Embassy instructions to stay put while their departure was being negotiated.

Compassionate as always, Shirley took it upon herself to reassure many terrified people that America cared, both for the Czech people and its own citizens. Connections to the outside world were few and hard to maintain, but Shirley recorded the names and hometowns of hotel guests (in addition to tourists and homeless people, the hotel was hosting an international conference of geologists) and spent hours on a pay telephone trying to disseminate information that people were safe. During the long three-and-a-half days holed up in the hotel, the staff continued to provide what meals

and other care they could, even as they discreetly expressed their support of their fallen leader, Alexander Dubček. Shirley was fascinated by the courage of the Czech youth, who were sneaking about and altering street signs in order to confuse the Soviet troops. Someone even put up a slogan sign that read, in Czech: HATE INTELLIGENTLY.

Word finally reached the hotel that the time was ripe for the American guests to board vehicles and begin to make their way to the embassy, where they would meet up with other groups of cars and slowly proceed through the town. The assemblage detoured through back streets to avoid tank blockades, but not all confrontations were avoidable. At one stop Shirley, in the lead car, waited for the driver to return and instead was given word to take the wheel herself. She began to drive as the convoy of over one hundred vehicles made its way to the outskirts of Prague. After several more hours of travel through the countryside, the Americans finally reached safety at the West German border. Reading Shirley's account, one can only wonder, as she did, what possessed the fleeing Americans—who frequently met up with Russian tanks along the way—to repeatedly call for comfort stops. The lights of one car would blink and all had to wait until that person was finished. But as Shirley had said before, one learns a lot about people by personal encounter. Not every individual is exemplary, such as the tourist who witnessed the death of a civilian in the hotel streetway and then brought home as a souvenir a bullet she rushed out to scoop up from the street. Or the one who paid extra to move to a room with a direct view of the street fighting.

ON THE FIFTH of September 1968, Shirley and Charles traveled overseas on a ten-day fundraising and voter-contact tour of Americans settled in Europe. The first destination was Rome, where Shirley held a press conference, threw a cocktail party fundraiser at the Hilton the next day, and entertained questions, including some snide ones from Italy's Communist paper. After a visit to the Borghese Gardens and a relaxing timeout for a puppet show, she and Charles headed on to France, West Germany, Spain, and finally England. "We hope to get at least ten thousand votes for [U.S.

The Shirley Temple Scrapbook

presidential candidate Richard] Nixon in Italy alone," she said.

Back in Germany again, there was a bit of levity when Shirley met U.S. Army Sergeant Shirley Temple Allanson, obviously named for the child star. Shirley consoled the sergeant with the news that her father had wanted to name her Beatrice. How much worse off he would have been with a name like that!

In London, Charles Black got off a memorable quote. "After twenty years," he said, "I'm used to public appreciation of my wife. I also share it."

Shirley's hard work in behalf of the GOP paid off, both locally and nationally. Not only did Richard Nixon defeat Democrat Hubert H. Humphrey in the presidential race, but many other Republicans won their respective House, Senate, and statewide contests.

IN THE LATE 1960s, Shirley served as a member of the U. S. Citizens Space Task Force. Chaired by the nation's vice president, the group met to discuss the future of the space program. The general consensus was that there should be some sort of unmanned space Grand Tour of the entire solar system and that a space station should then be planned and built. But now it was time to work on matters closer to home.

In 1969, President Nixon appointed Shirley Temple Black as a freshman delegate to the Twenty-fourth General Assembly of the United Nations, which seemed to follow the tradition that, in order to garner publicity, one U.S. delegate should have celebrity status. Shirley was assigned thirteen topics with which to become familiar—a hefty load. She later learned that the average workload was four. Although negative comments were made about her suitability for the job, Shirley was thrilled for the opportunity. She studied, listened, and prepared for whatever might be required, exhibiting a genuine desire to understand and shunning an interest in superficial matters, including the latest in fashion. Reporters frequently described her as dumpy or unglamorously dressed.

When Shirley Temple Black was sworn in as a UN delegate on September 16, 1969, the press remarked on her bright red suit while others noticed that all the cameras at the opening session were focused on her. Not just cameras. Nearly all the

delegates seemed to greet Shirley as an old friend. From the Iranian ambassador and the Shah of Iran to Carlos Romulo, Golda Meir, and UN Secretary General U Thant himself, everyone seemed to shower Shirley with love and respect. Angie Brooks gave her a great hug. Only Charles Yost, head of the U.S. delegation, sedately shook hands.

As Deputy Chairman of the United States Delegation to the United Nations Preparatory Committee for the First World Conference on Human Environment, Shirley delivered a speech to career UN diplomats. They were working for governments, she acknowledged, but in a larger sense they were working for the peoples of the world, born and unborn. She studied, mingled, discussed, and observed in the UN's halls and lounges and at cocktail parties. She was continually evaluating and negotiating. The $25.00 per day sum that Shirley was paid was no reflection of her ability or dedication. She quickly demonstrated that she was much more than window dressing.

Glen Olds, number-two man at the U.S. Mission to the UN, called Shirley the secret weapon of the United States. Her winning personality, overall preparedness, and willingness to share views impacted well on the attitudes of other delegates. They liked her a great deal, which meant that they would dislike the U.S. less. Regarding her relations with people from all over the world, Shirley summed it up concisely: "I'm a friend from their past and they trust me." She also learned what would be the cornerstone of her attitude toward foreign relations: Diplomacy is the art of persuasion. One important aspect of that art is humor, especially the ability to laugh at oneself.

Shirley's United Nations appointment was news worldwide. *Paris Match* gave her swearing-in a full-page picture, and Spain's *Hola!* Christmas issue devoted three pages to Shirley's work at the international body—and there was not a single child-star pose among them. That October, NBC's *Today* show interviewed Shirley about her new duties, and that was followed by a continuous round of receptions, conferences, and study to go along with the case of sinusitis she contracted after her arrival in New York.

It was with deserved joy that on December 9, 1969, having been named Woman of the Year at the

124

(Top) Shirley Temple Black, U. S. delegate to the United Nations, is seated in committee, alphabetically by country, just before the delegate from Upper Volta, Pierre Sanson. The date was September 30, 1969.

(Middle) On December 9, 1969, President Rex Wood of Sarah Coventry, the international jewelry firm, presented Shirley with its Woman of the Year Award for her distinguished public service as a United Nations delegate. On Shirley's left is the company's executive vice president, A. G. Winfrey.

(Right) Mr. and Mrs. Charles Black stand before the United States Mission to the UN. Shirley was one of ten U.S. delegates for the thirteen-week session.

U.S. Mission to the UN, Shirley received a small reward for her hard work: the Sarah Coventry Trophy. The previous year the award had gone to Pearl Buck.

In the summer of 1971, an exhibit of the Shirley Temple Black Collection of Dolls opened at the Children's Hospital at Stanford, in Palo Alto; Charles Black was the vice-president. The official preview of the event, sponsored by the Woodside-Atherton Auxiliary, was attended by sixteen consuls general, ten California city mayors, as well as the general public.

The doll collection was the topic of some discussion in a report by Pat Rogalla in *Rona Barrett's Hollywood*. According to the magazine, the collection was said to consist of fifteen hundred dolls. Shirley was presented with six more at the opening. By paring down, especially by donating duplicates to various children's hospitals in southern California, the collection was reduced to seven hundred sixty-one. However, some four hundred fifty of these were still in storage awaiting space to be displayed. Shirley, her parents, and the rest of the family—with the exception of young Charlie—were present at the doll collection opening.

Personal Challenges Award

The year 1972 was a momentous one for Shirley. UN conferences on the environment and world food problems took her to Stockholm, Cairo, and finally Moscow. That fall, at the White House, she was sworn in as Special Assistant to the Chairman of the President's Council on Environmental Quality. A biopsy of a lump in her breast, which had been delayed for six weeks due to travel obligations, was finally taken on November 2. The delay seemed of little consequence, and later Shirley refused to speculate on its impact.

Shirley decided to violate her rule of privacy and give full and detailed interviews regarding that biopsy and the breast cancer it revealed. The decision had been difficult, she admitted, and her years of acting experience didn't help her deal publicly with such a private matter. The family supported the decision to share.

In interviews and articles for movie and ladies' magazines, Shirley urged women to check regularly for lumps. She assured them that life after cancer was possible, even when surgery was necessary. Life, she stressed, is much more important than vanity. Those who until then were unconvinced that Shirley's real concern was human welfare quickly changed their minds. Women deluged her with letters expressing both their sympathy and gratitude for her speaking out on the importance of quality of life when there was so much emphasis on a woman's shape. The head and the heart, the mind and the spirit—these, not the bosom, shape a woman's life.

Although a March 1973 *Ladies' Circle* interview given at the Black residence devoted considerable space to describing home and furnishings, the February 1973 *McCall's* had concentrated on blunt factual details that would be helpful to others. Shirley presented information she had learned from her brother Jack, who was in hospital administration. European doctors, she recalled, no longer favored radical mastectomy, extensive research having found as high a survival rate and much better quality of life when less tissue is removed. Nonetheless, Shirley's specialists had asked for the standard procedure: biopsy, tissue analysis, and immediate radical treatment if cancer cells were present. She protested. Their suggested course, they insisted, would mean only one anesthesia instead of two—safer, quicker. But Shirley Temple Black was stubborn. She granted permission only for a biopsy. Lesser women would have been bullied into compliance—but not Shirley.

When cancer was found, the doctors recommended a modified radical mastectomy: removal of breast, lymph glands, and nodes under the arm. She again asserted her choice: removal of *only* the breast and a few lower nodes, a simple mastectomy. Thus, during surgery, only twelve of a possible eighty nodes were removed along with the breast. All of the nodes were found to be cancer-free. Shirley's *McCall's* interview stressed one overall point: It's your body. Find out the facts, then make your own choice.

On *The Mike Douglas Show*, Shirley reached out to women by telling her story and showing that undergoing a mastectomy was safe and lifesaving. She was sent to the UN, it was said, to cope with the world's traumas. Now she proved that she could cope with personal trauma as well—and that is always

On May 25, 1973, Shirley appeared on The Mike Douglas Show *to discuss her bout with breast cancer. Given the serious nature of the subject, the show's publicists were foolish to title it "On the Good Ship Douglas."*

the place to start. Shirley did turn down requests from cancer societies to join their volunteer forces; her heart still belonged to finding that cure for MS.

On May 28, 1974, Shirley was elected to the board of directors of Walt Disney Productions, becoming the first woman to hold the job. She was also a member of the board of Del Monte Corporation as well as a member of the United Nations Association, the National Wildlife Federation, and the National Multiple Sclerosis Society. A colorful paper feather headdress surfaced, printed with SHIRLEY TEMPLE FOR PRESIDENT. Shirley didn't need to run for that office. She was already First Lady many times over.

There had been many rumors, but at last, on September 12, 1974, *The Department of State Bulletin* confirmed that President Gerald R. Ford had appointed Shirley Temple Black as U.S. ambassador to the Republic of Ghana. Children Lori and

Charlie were in college, but husband Charles and daughter Susan accompanied the new ambassador to her post in Accra. On January 28, 1975, Shirley presented credentials to Ghana's head of state, Colonel Ignatius Kutu Acheampong, and stood under the traditional canopy of respect while a band played "The Star-Spangled Banner." This was answered with a welcome by Ghana's marvelous talking drums. At the embassy, Shirley assumed the responsibility of supervising seventy-seven staffers plus one hundred seventy-five Peace Corps volunteers and U.S. AID workers. The term of service was to be two years.

Ghana, a society in which women run the businesses and in which both inheritance and descent come through the mother, was genuinely honored that a top American woman was serving as ambassador. There was grumbling at the U.S. State Department, however, for there were those who considered the ambassadorship an honor suitable only for a man and a career diplomat . . . Well, Shirley had sat through fifty-five briefings on Ghana. Surely that counted for something!

In Ghana, Shirley and Susan toured the markets, met the women, and worked hard to set up women's and children's health clinics. Three months after Shirley's arrival, Colonel Acheampong declared the National Council on Women and Development an officially recognized organization. On women-owned Ghanaian taxicabs, signs carried a slogan that translated to: FEAR WOMEN! Women had power.

> The staff at the American Embassy in Ghana consisted of about fourteen people. Among them was Shirley's deputy prime minister, a man she later described as very tall and given to crossing his legs when he sat. Obviously, the deputy had not been adequately briefed that one did not do this in the presence of a chief, of which Ghana had many. An even worse insult was to show the bottom of one's foot. When, on one occasion, Shirley and her deputy were calling on a chief, the deputy sat with his legs crossed. Not only that, but his shoe sole was beginning to appear. Frantically, Shirley tried to gesture to the deputy to lower his foot, but in her confusion she missed a question from the chief via a translator and absently replied with a yes. She had just agreed to join his two present wives by marrying him. A good bit of diplomacy was required to handle the situation.

Shirley herself was not to be feared. When the Yugoslav ambassador to Ghana called on her, she served him hot bouillon rather than coffee. He loved it and asked for a supply for his residence. She played ping-pong with the Chinese ambassador, chess with the Russian—and, in losing to both, won better relations. Charles traveled in and out of the country, attending to his work for Mardela (Marine Research Development Corporation) on the culture and preparation of fish varieties to improve food supplies, but avoiding any hint that he was using her position. He accompanied Shirley to official functions, and he and Susan substituted for

her on occasion. Susan also found time to indulge her interest in travel and writing, then she fell in love with the first secretary at the Italian Embassy, Roberto Falaschi. For her part, Shirley also worked to help U.S. firms already partnering with Ghanaian business, including the Kaiser-Reynolds aluminum plant and the Firestone Rubber Plantation and Tire Factory. She hoped to encourage more such partnerships.

LINDA SUSAN BLACK married her Italian sweetheart, but Ambassador Shirley Temple Black's stay in Ghana did not last the two years. President Ford rated her first-class, and Henry Kissinger described her as terrific. But there was a controversial happening not of her making that in July 1976 led to President Ford's asking Shirley to relinquish her position. The incident apparently involved a visit by Secretary of State Henry Kissinger to pro-American states in the area, but Ghana was not included. Shirley pressed him to visit that country and appealed to Ghana to extend an invitation, but Communist influences vetoed the idea. Shirley had pushed for a friendship into which the U.S. wasn't prepared to enter or the Marxists to risk.

Shirley acceded to President Ford's request, but that did not mean that Ghana would no longer be in her heart and thoughts. When, in a 1982 interview, she was asked about the country's latest coup, she responded that she wasn't privy to details, but that every time there was another coup—and this was the second in two years—it set the country back five to ten years economically, for all loans and aid were cut off until a stable government was again in control. The interview made it clear that although Shirley's tenure in Ghana had ended years earlier, she brought a fondness for the country home with her. She also brought home a dog.

Soon after Shirley's return to the U.S., President Ford appointed her chief of protocol, the first woman to hold this assistant secretary of state position, and on August 20, 1976, she was sworn in.

A British newspaper used this portrait of "Little Miss Ambassador" in its Sunday magazine section. Unfortunately, it still had to include a child star photo.

The television newsmagazine 60 Minutes showed Shirley presenting credentials in Ghana on January 28, 1975. In formal coat and gloves, she certainly needed the shade of the canopy.

Always an essential member of the team, Charles joined Shirley in a sublet apartment in Washington, D.C., regularly returning home there from his worldwide fisheries efforts.

Now Shirley had a staff of forty-four to help her welcome visiting heads of state, meeting each at point of entry and assisting until departure. She saw to cars and other needs: real estate, immunity, parking, threats, as well as anything else required by the foreign diplomats at the one hundred twenty-five embassies. A head of state or foreign leader was hosted for six days at U.S. expense; each was permitted to bring in eleven people, whom the U.S. housed and entertained. Shirley oversaw all arrangements.

Fortunately for Shirley, the embassy staff included knowledgeable locals. One evening, Shirley was sure she heard a poor little kitten crying in the lovely embassy garden and went hunting it. She bent over, intending to pick it up, when the gardener grabbed her arm. This was no kitten, he explained, but the wail of a poisonous snake. The garden also yielded a cobra and a puff adder. One was not supposed to go outside in the cool of the evening. That was when the snakes loved to roam.

She also acted as chief of protocol for the White House, which involved making arrangements when the President traveled abroad. She coordinated various national festival day celebrations and was in charge of Blair House, the official guest residence. With all of her versatility, and despite the fact that she worked extremely long hours, there was one important job that Shirley could not fill, that of wife to the chief of protocol. Because she was a woman, the men expected her to fetch coffee; she solved that by having coffee ready ahead of time. The wife of one head of state even asked Shirley to do her hair. The long series of unexpected tasks culminated in Shirley's making arrangements for the inauguration of Democrat President Jimmy Carter.

Following Carter's assumption of the presidency, Shirley offered to stay and continue to serve her country, but was declined. Three days later, with the inauguration festivities concluded, Shirley Temple Black was dismissed.

On January 1, 1977, Gertrude Temple died. Shirley shared no details and mourned in private. George Temple continued to live in a wing of the Woodside home.

AFTER LEAVING GOVERNMENT service, Shirley traveled with Charles a great deal, assuming secretarial duties. Much of his work involved expanding food resources in developing countries. As tape recorders were largely unknown and suspect, Shirley took notes in longhand, often for hours at a time. Charles was highly dedicated to his work, and soon he became an important member of the National Atmospheric and Oceanographic Agency in the field of marine mammals.

In 1977, Shirley received an official invitation to visit China from that government's foreign ministry. Perhaps this was an outgrowth of exchanges she had with the Chinese ambassador to Ghana. Or perhaps the Chinese recalled when, as chief of protocol, Shirley had invited a group of their diplomats to Blair House for dessert and a film showing of *Stowaway*. At first the Chinese had been distrustful, phoning several times to inquire whether the film was propaganda. Ultimately, after accepting her disclaimers and attending the showing, the Chinese were pleasantly surprised—not so much for the set decoration or even that some Chinese was accurately spoken, but that little Shirley spoke Mandarin. So now, as a mature adult, Shirley would be heading to China for several months.

China was filled with surprises. While observing a hydroelectric dam at a fair in Guangzhou, Shirley felt a tap on the shoulder. It was Bessie Nyi, the teacher who had taught Shirley all that Mandarin for *Stowaway*. What a joyous reunion! Newspapers reported Shirley's return home to the United States on December 16, 1977.

With the next year, 1978, came more travel, conferences, and other meetings dealing with health and environmental issues. Shirley drove herself hard. Among the highlights was attending the

Homecoming at the Westlake School for Girls. Achievement Awards were given to Eleanor Richards Lyon, class of 1908; Shirley Temple Black, class of 1945; and astronaut Sally Ride, class of 1968.

In between her European travels, Shirley's father died and she bid him a quiet goodbye. Then, on December 30, 1980, she extended a joyous hello to newborn granddaughter Theresa Falaschi. Early in 1981, Shirley and Charles were honored guests at the European Inauguration Ball for President Ronald Reagan, held in Paris. They flew home the next day, only to have Shirley asked to go to Geneva to attend the International Conference on African Refugees. Later, she was sent to Europe for a tour with NATO. Her involvement in foreign affairs kept her busy outside the country.

Then Shirley accepted a special job with Ambassador Dean Brown, a foreign-affairs officer. Starting in April 1981, working under the U.S. State Department, Ambassadors Brown and Black (her title is for life) set up a series of three-day seminars for new ambassadors and their wives. Instruction covered the functions of the embassy, the restrictions under which it operates, and what its personnel can do for U.S. nationals living in foreign countries as well as for local citizens. The ambassadors were given important tips on managing a mission, maximizing use of their own time, and adjusting to local ways. Shirley focused on the issue of political appointees, and she had plenty of funny and scary stories to tell.

Shirley held memberships in more organizations than a lesser person could keep track of. In 1984, as president of San Francisco's Commonwealth Club, she welcomed French President François Mitterand, introducing him as the club's March 28 speaker. Generally, Commonwealth Club events included discussions of ballot measures, luncheons and receptions for important speakers, and local and worldwide tours. As president, Shirley signed membership cards and letters to members urging them to sign up friends. Alas, she must have nearly fainted when a letter with her signature announced a forthcoming speaker from the State Department, incorrectly spelling the name of her good friend Henry Kissinger as Henry Kissenger.

At the 1984 Academy Awards ceremony, held

Shirley was presented with a 1978 Achievement Award at the Westlake School for Girls Homecoming.

on April 9, Shirley helped celebrate the fiftieth anniversary of the creation of Donald Duck, with whom she had appeared in one cartoon, Disney's 1939 *The Autograph Hound.* A group of her own film clips was shown. Then Shirley displayed the baby Oscar she had received many years earlier. She reminisced about her career, finishing with a question to Johnny Carson that harkened back to the original ceremony: "Johnny, can I go home now?"

On May 20, 1985, the Academy Foundation sponsored "A Tribute to Shirley Temple" at the Academy's Sam Goldwyn Theater, with Robert Osborne serving as the evening's moderator. At the tribute (tickets were $5.00 for the public and $2.00 for Academy members), film clips of Shirley's performances were interspersed with the recollections

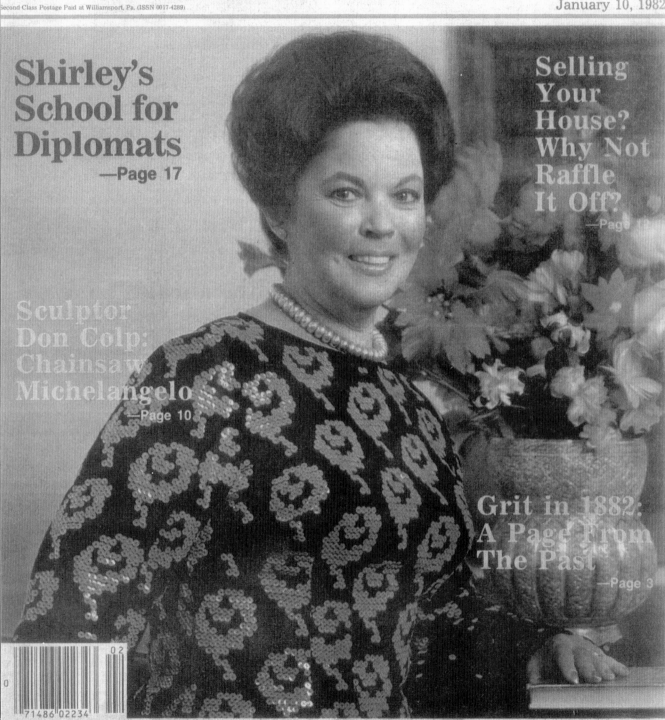

GRIT

AMERICA'S FAMILY NEWSPAPER

45 Cents

January 10, 1982

Second Class Postage Paid at Williamsport, Pa. (ISSN 0017-4289)

Shirley's School for Diplomats
—Page 17

Selling Your House? Why Not Raffle It Off?
—Page

Sculptor Don Colp: Chainsaw Michelangelo
—Page 10

Grit in 1882: A Page From The Past
—Page 3

The January 10, 1982, issue of Grit *carried this cover of ambassador-teacher Black.*

of Shirley and her various costars. She had recently donated to the Academy archives some home movies made by her mother during the filming of *Heidi*, a few of which were also shown. At the close, Gene Allen presented Shirley with a full-size Oscar. This was accompanied by the admission that the special miniature award had been created because the adult stars could not tolerate the idea of competing against Shirley or any other child star.

Jane Withers flew in from New York for the tribute and, judging from reporters' accounts, when she did her Shirley Temple imitation, Shirley was not amused. As would any proud husband, Charles Black videotaped the entire proceeding. Shirley introduced him and Susan (Lori and Charles Jr. were otherwise engaged), as well as her two brothers, George Jr. and Jack. She spoke briefly about her work as Chief of Protocol, then sang one of her old songs, "How Can I Thank You?" Before anyone realized it, she had slipped out through a side door. Later in 1985, beloved brother Jack died. The Academy tribute was the last special event at which he would treasure his little sister.

The Brown and Black training seminars that were begun in 1981 grew into the American Academy of Diplomacy in 1986. By then, Shirley had participated in five years of seminars, having trained one hundred forty-two first-time ambassadors and spouses.

Shirley greets people at the 1985 tribute during which the Motion Picture Academy gave her a long overdue (by fifty years) full-size Oscar.

AS ONE STUDIES various Shirley interviews, further bits of information about her life and service invariably come to light. In *Parade* magazine of December 7, 1986, Shirley reminisced about her early years. Interviewers nearly always focused on her film career as though the rest of Shirley's life were a pigtail added to her little-girl curls. She spoke of her mother as shy, but skillful in dealing with plumbing, electrical work, and, of course, sewing clothes.

The *Parade* article also revealed that although Shirley's maternal grandmother, Maude Cregier, was a steady smoker, Shirley actually picked up the lifelong habit while a student at the Westlake School for Girls. Before attending Westlake, she confided, she had been shielded from both profanity and off-color language. And, she further confided, she had been engaged to be engaged to seven servicemen before meeting John Agar and taking the situation seriously.

By the time of publication of the *Parade* article, Shirley was working on her autobiography, which would be published in 1988 with the title *Child Star*. Initially, Shirley intended for the book to focus only on family. She had her mother's diary plus her own memories, and scrapbooks loaded with countless clippings. Shirley wrote in longhand, a tedious process that may inadvertently account for her sharing some details of her life.

On January 30, 1988, the American Cinema Awards Foundation held its fifth annual awards fundraiser to benefit the Motion Picture and TV Country Home and Hospital in Woodland Hills, California. Awards went to Gene Kelly and Shirley,

(Left) When Child Star *was published in 1988, Shirley made many bookstore appearances to meet fans and autograph copies of her life story. This photo was taken in Philadelphia.*

(Opposite) *Shirley Temple Black and granddaughter Teresa Falaschi, age eight, pose for the cover of the Television Times section of the* Los Angeles Times *to announce Shirley's return as Grand Marshal of the Rose Parade.*

plus to Janet Jackson as recording performer of the year. Organized by David Guest, it drew some three hundred celebrities, each of whom was named and asked to stand and be acknowledged. It was a long night!

The New Year of 1989 saw Shirley return to the Tournament of Roses. She had been Grand Marshal of the fiftieth anniversary Rose Parade in 1939. Now she returned for the one hundredth anniversary. Although a very private person, her joy over granddaughter Teresa Falaschi, Susan's girl, was evidenced by her willingness to share pictures and her general air of grandmotherly delight. With New Year's Day coming on Sunday, the Tournament of Roses Parade was held on Monday, January 2. Interestingly, Shirley revealed that she was allergic to red roses, so she was surrounded with other colors. Riding with her on the float was eight-year-old Teresa. Tournament president John H. Biggar III said Shirley was perfect for the centennial because she represents the Tournament tradition of celebrating life and family, and of living for the present, enjoying the past, and planning for the future.

In keeping with the theme of drawing from the past and building for the future, President George H. Bush appointed Shirley as ambassador to Czechoslovakia on June 1, 1989. Given the title of Ambassador Extraordinary and Plenipotentiary of the United States of America to the Czechoslovak Socialist Republic, she replaced Julian Martin Niemczyk, serving from 1989 to 1992.

It was an uneasy time, for Shirley's sympathy and interest were with the oppressed, and she wanted to discover how old Czech friends had fared. She evaded the secret police to sneak into an antigovernment rally of students in Prague's Wenceslas Square. The protestors demanded free elections, and she and Charles left the protest just as riot cops erected barricades. From a filthy window ledge in a friend's apartment, she watched what she termed the Velvet Revolution. A few days later, the Communist Party paper commented that the American ambassador had been seen on a balcony reserved to watch such events. Fortunately, the location was incorrectly identified by Shirley. She hoped for no repercussions for the friend.

Ambassador Black regularly met with Czech government representatives who requested Most Favored Nation status, which would lower tariffs on Czech exports to the United States and thus lead to increased sales. She would counter by presenting lists of human-rights grievances and names of political prisoners. But her efforts were to no avail. Instead, results came when Hungary, Poland, and East Germany moved towards democracy. As in the earlier demonstration, Czech students massed to

TELEVISION TIMES

Shirley Temple Black
pays a return visit to the
Rose Parade

demand elections. The police retaliated savagely. Fed up at last, the Czech people reacted strongly but nonviolently, toppling the Communist government.

During her time in Czechoslovakia, Shirley had gotten to know important nationals. Now, in freedom, she welcomed back film director Milos Forman with a party that included Václav Havel, soon to become the first non-Communist president of that land in forty years. She began meeting with the new government leaders, arranging exchanges between U.S. senators and representatives. No wonder the U.S. State Department officials named her its first honorary Foreign Service Officer.

There were more honors. In March of 1998, the Academy Awards honored Shirley Temple Black's life and achievements. Writeups commented that son Charlie, at the age of forty-six, was a Bay Area business consultant; that Lori, at age forty-four, was a photographer and musician; that granddaughter Teresa was now seventeen; and that Teresa's mother, Susan, now divorced, was a high-school librarian. There was the sad yet amazing note that brother George had only succumbed to multiple sclerosis in 1995. His long survival was a great encouragement to many others with the disease.

On December 7, 1998, Shirley became one of those esteemed Americans to be awarded the Kennedy Center Honors, its twenty-first such presentation.

The year 2000 saw Shirley cooking Thanksgiving dinner for the entire family. One month later, she and Charles celebrated fifty years of marriage.

New Generations, New Admirers

As the twentieth century drew to a close, an assortment of audio recordings featuring songs from Shirley Temple film soundtracks and videos of the films themselves were issued. As it had when Shirley's films were shown on television, Twentieth Century-Fox arranged for the releases, did publicity using her photos, and pocketed all the profits. Photographs and films carried the studio copyright,

but there was also the credit: OFFICIALLY AUTHORIZED BY SHIRLEY TEMPLE.

With the periodic release of new Shirley Temple dolls throughout the 1990s, Shirley began to exert her own rights to face and name. The Dress-Up Doll, a series of reproductions of movie outfits sent every other month to fit a sixteen-inch vinyl doll, was free with the series. Arrangements with the Danbury Mint brought out plates and figurines depicting Shirley's movie roles. There were porcelain collector dolls personally authorized by Shirley and made by artist Elke Hutchens—a 17.5-inch *Curly Top* bride and a 10.5-inch *Baby Take a Bow* doll among them. The first porcelain creation had been a 1986 *Stand Up and Cheer* doll officially authorized by Shirley Temple Black.

In the year 2000, Little Miss Shirley Toddler, a doll seated eleven inches high, again designed by Hutchens, was put on the market. About the same time, Danbury released a five-piece (two lids) porcelain tea set with artist portraits of the 1934 gardener Shirley in blue coveralls.

SHIRLEY TEMPLE continues to fascinate and intrigue, just as she continues to be big business. With each new release of a film or a doll, more older people become captivated by the happy face they have loved for so long and decide to join the rank of collector. As young people discover the joy of Shirley Temple for the first time, they, too, become Shirley followers. Meanwhile, Shirley Temple Black continues to dedicate herself to the improvement of world health and the environment.

Irvin S. Cobb was so right when long ago he described little Shirley as Santa's greatest gift to mankind. But, considering what she has bestowed upon the world, it would be equally appropriate to equate Shirley with Santa himself. As an adorable child blessed with a magical talent, Shirley gave joy to countless millions. As a concerned and compassionate adult, Shirley Temple Black continues to brighten the world by promoting peace, understanding, and respect between peoples everywhere. An enormous gift indeed.

Part Two

THE FILMS

1932

The Runt Page *had Shirley as a newspaper columnist, busy and butting into the lives of others.*

LULU PARSNIPS

THE RUNT PAGE

Educational Films Corp., subsidiary of Educational Pictures, Inc.

Shirley Temple appeared in a series of short subjects called Baby Burlesks, which featured small children under three feet tall. The Baby Stars, as they were known, were costumed in diapers, further emphasizing the studio's intent: to make silly fun of serious films. With each running about ten minutes, the Baby Burlesks were designed to fill in a theater's bill along with cartoons and some news or educational reels.

The first Burlesk, made in January 1932, was a spoof of *The Front Page*, a newspaper story. It may not have been in general release until after Educational's assets were sold following bankruptcy.

Shirley Temple .... Lulu Parsnips (Louella Parsons)
Georgie Smith ....Raymond Bunion (Damon Runyon)
Unknown player Bears Bugs .... (Arthur "Bugs" Baer)

Directed by Roy Laverne
Produced by Jack Hays

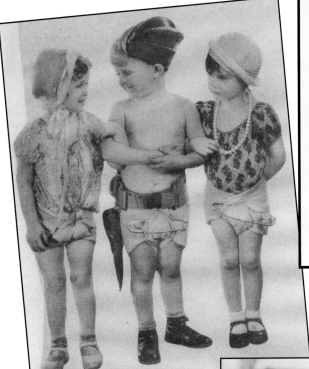

WAR BABIES

Educational Films Corp.; production #321001 or 1207 or 0701, depending on release dates.*

A spoof of the classic war film *What Price Glory?*, the plot of this Baby Burlesk was reduced to soldiers coming to a milk bar for drinks and to meet girls, especially little vamp Shirley.

Shirley Temple .... Charmaine, a French girl
Georgie Smith .... soldier boyfriend
Eugene Butler .... soldier boyfriend
Lou Ann Jones .... bar girl
Mary Howard .... bar girl

Musical director: Lee Zahler
Recording engineer: W. C. Smith
Directed by Charles Lamont
Produced by Jack Hays

Shirley's competition for the affections of the soldiers is Lou Ann Jones and Mary Howard. Here, Georgie Smith debates.

In War Babies, *entertainer Shirley welcomes doughboys Georgie Smith and Eugene Butler. She is a convincing flirt.*

* Production numbers and dates are provided where verifiable.

*Here's Shirley, the winner,
with hands on hips . . .*

*. . . What is Shirley's reward?
A hug and a kiss.*

*Publicity for the film had the Baby Stars
heralding Kellogg's Corn Flakes. This was
not part of the film itself.*

This pensive pose from The Pie-Covered Wagon *shows Shirley's expressive eyes rather than her infectious smile. The dog is also thoughtful.*

THE PIE-COVERED WAGON

Educational Films Corp; production #321002.

Unlike *The Covered Wagon*, which it spoofed, *The Pie-Covered Wagon* featured unnamed characters. True to its title, the film's ammunition was pies—real ones of several flavors.

Shirley Temple
Georgie Smith
Cowboys and Indians
Directed by Charles Lamont
Written and produced by Jack Hays

Hero of the Wagon *spoof, Georgie rescues Shirley from the Indians.*

Shirley is baffled by the assortment of Indians who captured her from the wagon train.

Union Films, Inc., compiled various film comedy sequences into their feature The Sound of Laughter. *This bit shows* Glad Rags *Shirley, her patient maid, and her pin-up boy, Georgie, from an earlier Burlesk.*

Unhappy but rich, Shirley is helped into a cape by her maid.

GLAD RAGS TO RICHES

Educational Films Corp.; production #321003.

This was a satire of the "rags to riches" and "discovered star" movie genres, which included such films as *Dinner at Eight* and *A Star Is Born*. The poor but pretty girl who went from rags to riches is Shirley, who sang her first film song, "She's Only a Bird in a Gilded Cage," in the release.

Shirley Temple .... La Belle Diaperina, showgirl
Eugene Butler .... her employer
Marilyn Granas .... girl (later Shirley's first stand-in)
Georgie Smith .... Elmer, Shirley's country sweetheart

Directed by Charles Lamont
Produced by Jack Hays

A sober Shirley wears an impressive outfit in Glad Rags to Riches. *One misses a lot in having to view these Burlesks in current poor-quality prints.*

Girlfriend Shirley, showing some concern and wearing rather dowdy clothes, watches her boxing champ hoist a few weights.

THE KID'S LAST STAND

Educational Films Corp.; production #321004

Also known as *The Kid's Last Fight*, in this film the world of boxing was ridiculed, or just imitated, since thugs kidnapped the boxer's girlfriend and tried to force him to throw the championship fight. The girlfriend, Shirley, was saved just in time, but in real life she was actually rescued due to having eaten some green apples during filming. According to Jack Hays, ambulances from three hospitals came to their aid.

Shirley Temple .... the girlfriend
Georgie Smith .... Diaper Dampsy (Jack Dempsey)
Sidney Kilbrick .... a thug

Directed by Charles Lamont
Produced by Jack Hays

KIDDIN' HOLLYWOOD

Educational Films Corp.; production #321005.

In this movieland spoof, Shirley won a beauty contest, but the only work she could get at the studio was scrubbing floors. When a temperamental superstar was too bored and tired to film, she was replaced by Shirley. As with *The Runt Page*, this film may have crossed the line from satire to insult in its depictions of Greta Garbo, Marlene Dietrich, and Erich von Stroheim. The three Yes Men were also a real—and deserved—crack at the studios in general. As Dietrich, Shirley sang "We Just Couldn't Say Good-bye."

Shirley Temple .... Morelegs Sweetrick
Georgie Smith .... Frightwig von Stumblebum
Gloria Ann Mack .... Freta Snobo

Directed by Charles Lamont
Produced by Jack Hays

Shirley has won a beauty contest out in the sticks and comes to Hollywood to make it in the movies, bringing her prize cup along.

(Opposite) Jack Hays shows Shirley just where to fix her eyes to convey the proper sultry feeling. Despite the fact that Lamont received directorial credit, this plainly demonstrates that Jack Hays was truly in charge.

146

Georgie Smith greets his star while Shirley, as Morelegs Sweetrick, shows her legs and gives Georgie her best "Come hither!" look.

(Opposite) Shirley and Georgie pose at Grauman's Chinese Theatre just above the footprints of Douglas Fairbanks, but in the film Kiddin' Hollywood star Shirley was a failure. Just three years later, her prints would be here.

POLLY-TIX IN WASHINGTON

Educational Films Corp.; production #321006.

This depiction of the Washington political scene saw Shirley in the role of a seductress seeking to repay favorable votes. Her two-piece black lace undies were very provocative, and Gloria Ann Mack, playing the hick senator's daughter, got Shirley's *Wagon* hand-me-downs.

Shirley Temple .... a political golddigger
Georgie Smith .... cowboy novice politician
Gloria Ann Mack .... his defensive daughter

Western Electric recording
Sound engineer: W. S. Smith
Musical director: Alfonso Corelli
Photographed by Dwight Warren
Directed by Charles Lamont

Here, Shirley gets a phone call from her boss asking her to go and vamp a new senator into signing a bill. The set is carefully decorated; so is Shirley, in an outfit such as adult stars were wearing. Censor Will Hays would soon restrict undies poses. The little maid never got the screen credit she deserved.

(Opposite) Dedicated senator Georgie Smith and daughter Gloria Ann Mack (aka White) join Shirley and a congressional aide in a wagon not used in the Polly-Tix *film.*

1933

KIDDIN' AFRICA

Educational Films Corp.; production #321007; also #0701 for release with a Frolics of Youth series.

This parody of Tarzan films included a missionary lady and cannibals. It also spoofed some of the early liberated woman films by having Shirley marry Tarzan and then have him doing dishes.

Shirley Temple ...... Madame Cradlebait, missionary who became Mrs. Diaperzan
Danny Boone, Jr. .... Diaperzan
Unnamed .... cannibals and a preacher man

Shirley's pose to announce her missionary expedition in Kiddin' Africa *reminds one of many other explorers setting out with big ideas—and publicity. These porters later doubled as cannibals.*

(Opposite) Tarzan's tree was scratchy, and both Shirley and Danny Boone, Jr., pose sitting on towel padding. The film is Kiddin' Africa, *but Shirley is all business.*

Myrna Kennedy meets Shirley, daughter of her accused boyfriend. She defends him for the sake of his irresistible child.

THE RED-HAIRED ALIBI

Tower Productions, Inc.; production #RHA.

A man in trouble with the law has a girlfriend who becomes his alibi when she gets interested in his little girl, played by Shirley. Shirley's sequences were released as 16mm films and as tiny strips for toy viewers after Shirley became famous.

Myrna Kennedy .... Lynn Monith	Marion Lessing .... Bee Lee
Theo. von Eltz .... Trent Travers (Eltz)	Shirley Temple .... Gloria Shelton
Grant Withers .... Bob Shelton	Paul Porcasi .... Margoli
Parnell Pratt .... Regan	Arthur Hoyt .... Henri
Huntley Gordon .... Kente	
Fred Kelsey .... Corcoran	
John Vosburgh .... Morgan	

Story by Wilson Collison
Screenplay by Edward T. Lowe
Directed by Christy Cabanne

Teacher Andy Clyde "tests" Shirley to sing on the radio. She suddenly gets mike fright.

DORA'S DUNKING DOUGHNUTS

Educational Films Corp.; production #3210108 and 0202.

Educational Studios evidently felt the need—or the Hays Office censor pressured them—to produce more wholesome, less risqué film shorts. The result was a series of releases known as the Frolics of Youth, of which *Dora's Dunking Doughnuts* was one.

   The Frolics were young teen comedies in which Shirley sometimes was featured as the only small child. Andy Clyde, an established comedian who had made short subjects for Educational, also sometimes appeared. *Dora's* was billed as both an Andy Clyde Comedy and a Frolic of Youth, but in both cases Shirley got top billing.

   Dora's Dunking Doughnuts tells of a financially troubled doughnut shop operated by Andy's beloved, Dora. Andy tries to help Dora by advertising on the radio, but the radio program, featuring schoolchildren, is disastrous. It is Dora's new invention—a Dunking Doughnut that quickly sponges up liquid—that becomes a big seller and saves the shop.

Andy Clyde .... Andrew Wilson, teacher
Ethel Sykes ...... Miss Dora, doughnut inventor
Shirley Temple .... Shirley
Bud Jaimison .... radio manager
Bille Engle .... radio announcer
Florence Gill .... The Barnyard Nightingale
Fern Emmett .... Mrs. Zilch

Blanche Payson .... Mrs. Blotts
Georgia O'Dell .... Mrs. Ipswick
The Meglin Kids Band

Story and dialogue by Ernest Pagano
and Ewart Adamson
Musical numbers by Alfonse Corelli
Directed by Harry J. Edwards

Between scenes, Shirley and Andy have fun in the sun reviewing the silly script.

All of Andy's schoolchildren love Dora's shop. Andy loves Dora. Notice all the product tie-ups. After shooting, everyone would eat these props.

The children are rewarded for trying to help Dora. They celebrate her success—but they must be eating up all the profits!

OUT ALL NIGHT

Universal, May 1933; production #625

In this feature film, Slim Summerville is forced to take his mother along on his honeymoon. Comedy sequences show him gradually cutting the apron strings. Since the Educational Burlesks and Frolics were made through arrangement with Universal, Jack Hays supplied Shirley for this feature.

Slim Summerville .... Ronald Colgate
ZaSu Pitts .... Bonny, the bride
Laura Hope Crews .... Mrs. Colgate, the mother
Shirley Grey .... Kate
Alexander Carr .... Rosemountain
Rollo Lloyd .... Arnold
Billy Barty, Shirley Temple, Phillip Purdy .... children
Gene Lewis .... Tracy
Also: Florence Enright, Dorothy Bay, Mae Busch, Paul Hurst

Story by Tim Whelan
Screenplay by William Anthony McGuire
Directed by Sam Taylor

MERRILY YOURS

Educational Films Corp.; Frolics production #0303

This comedy saw Shirley as a little sister who disrupts her brother's chores. He is in a hurry to take his new girlfriend to a dance and keep her out of the clutches of a big-time operator. When filming began at the end of summer 1933, Shirley's salary was then up to $15.00 a day.

Junior Coughlin or Coghlan .... Sonny Rogers
Kenneth Howell .... Harry Vanderpool
Shirley Temple .... Mary Lou Rogers
Sidney Miller .... Harry's "stooge"
Harry Myers .... Mr. Rogers
Helene Chadwick .... Mrs. Rogers
Lloyd Ingraham... Mr. Dean
Thelma Hill .... Betty
Isabel La Mal .... Mrs. Vanderpool

Photographed by Dwight Warren
Western Electric Noiseless Recording
Written and directed by Charles Lamont

Poor Junior Coughlin gets
scolded by Isabel La Mal for
doing a poor job of raking
leaves. Innocent-looking Shirley
is the real culprit.

Despite all the problems, big
brother Junior loves little
sister Shirley, but of course
she is sweet when asleep.

PARDON MY PUPS

Educational Films Corp.; Frolics production #0310

Sonny rescues a dog found under the bridge and is determined to keep it, even though Harry claims that it's his. They fight over the dog, which has enough pups for everyone.

Frank (Junior) Coughlin	Sonny Rogers
Shirley Temple	Mary Lou Rogers
Kenneth Howell	Harry Vanderpool
Dorothy Ward	Mrs. Rogers
Harry Myers	Mr. Rogers
Virginia True Boardman	Sonny's girlfriend
Queenie	the spaniel

Suggested by the story "Mild Oats," by Florence Ryerson
and Colin Clements
Story adapted by Ewart Adamson
Directed by Charles Lamont

(Above) Shirley comes to Junior's bed to wake him, teasing him with a feather.

(Opposite, top) Shirley is a bit uneasy about feeding the dog a plate of spaghetti after they have tended to its wounds. She was justified: the dog unraveled Sonny's sweater and ate it along with the spaghetti. The pups were born wearing little sweaters.

(Opposite, below) Kenneth is angry that Junior has rescued the dog and fights to get her back. Shirley defends Junior with a fork to Kenneth's backside—and the fork promptly bends.

MANAGED MONEY

Educational Films Corp.; Frolics production #0313

Junior wants to attend military school with his pal, but the family can't afford that. He and his pal go prospecting, hoping to strike it rich. Shirley sneaks along and rescues a stranger who turns out to be the military school owner. Naturally, Junior is enrolled.

Frank (Junior) Coughlin .... Sonny Rogers
Shirley Temple .... Mary Lou Rogers
Harry Myers .... Mr. Rogers
Huntly Gordon .... school owner

Story and dialogue by Ernest Pagano and Ewart Adamson
Directed by Charles Lamont

Managed Money *comes to a happy ending when Junior and his friend are enrolled in military school. Shirley saved the day—and the school's owner. School scenes were shot at Hollywood's Black-Foxe Military Institute.*

(Opposite) Copy of a rare one-sheet poster for Managed Money.

WHAT TO DO?

Educational Films Corp.; a Frolics production.

Just when Junior and his baseball team are playing for the championship, his father announces a sudden move to another town. Junior feigns illness to delay the move, but little sister Shirley contests his every effort by exposing the fakery.

As a direct tie-up, the pressbook for this Frolic announced that the Los Angeles Doll Company "is manufacturing dolls, modeled from a number of our Baby Stars. A doll of the beautiful Shirley Temple is now ready." None has yet been identified with certainty.

Frank (Junior) Coughlin .... Sonny Rogers
Shirley Temple .... Mary Lou Rogers
Harry Myers .... Mr. Rogers
Kenneth Howell .... Harry Vanderpool
Lila Leslie.. Dorothy Ward
(discovered for this
by Phyllis Haver)

Also: Broderick O'Farrell

TO THE LAST MAN

Paramount; December 1933 release; production #1455.

This Zane Grey feature combined a multigenerational feud with a western range war. Children from the two feuding families grew up to love each other and, finally, secure a truce.

Randolph Scott .... Lynn Hayden
Esther Ralston .... Ellen Colby
Shirley Jane Temple .... Mary Standing
Buster Crabbe .... Bill Hayden
Noah Beery .... Jed Colby
Jack LaRue .... Jim Daggs
Barton MacLaine .... Neil Standing
Gail Patrick .... Ann Hayden (Shirley's mother)
Egon Brecher .... Mark Hayden
Fuzzy Knight .... Jeff Morley
James Engles .... Ely Bruce
Murial Kirkland .... Molly Hayden
Eugenie Besserer .... Granny Spelvin
Harlan Knight................................. Grandpa Spelvin
John Peter Richmond .... Pete Garon
Harry Cording .... Harry Malone
Erville Anderson .... Judge
James Burke .... Sheriff
Jay Ward .... Lynn Hayden as a child
Rosita Butler .... Ann Hayden as a child
Cullen Johnson...................... Bill Hayden as a child
Russell Powell .... Greaves
Delmar Watson .... Ted Standing

Adapted from the book by Zane Grey
Directed by Henry Hathaway

CAROLINA

Fox Film Corp.; February 1934; production #133.

The downfall of an old Southern aristocratic family is dramatized in the clash between Yankee and rebel generals. The cast list, as given in the April 1934 issue of *Photoplay*, contained no mention of Shirley, who played a sharecropper's daughter.

Janet Gaynor .... Joanna
Lionel Barrymore .... Bob Connelly
Robert Young .... Will Connelly
Richard Cromwell .... Allen
Mona Barrie .... Virginia
Stepin Fetchitt .... Scipio
Russell Simpson .... Richards
Ronnie Crosby .... Harry
Jackie Cosbey .... Jackie
Almeda Fowler .... Geraldine
Alden Chase .... Jack Hampton
Roy Watson .... Jefferson Davis
John Elliott .... General Robert E. Lee
John Webb Dillon .... General "Stonewall" Jackson
J. C. Fowler .... General Leonidas Polk
Andre Cheron .... General Beauregard

Based on the story "The House of Connelly," by Paul Green
Screenplay by Reginald Berkeley
Directed by Henry King

MANDALAY

First National; February-March 1934.

The heroine, played by Kay Francis, has two suitors. Suspense builds to the point where she murders the bad guy, Ricardo Cortez, so as to reach the happy ending. In Great Britain the film was considered a violation of the "purity pash," the derisive British term for the new U.S. passion for purity as represented by censor Will Hays.

Kay Francis .... Tanya
Ricardo Cortez .... Tony Evans
Warner Oland .... Nick
Lyle Talbott .... Dr. Gregory Burton
Ruth Donnelly .... Mrs. Peters
Reginald Owen .... police captain
Hobart Cavanaugh .... purser
David Torrence .... captain
Rafaela Ottiano .... the Countess
Holliwell Hobbes .... Colonel Dawson Ames
Etienne Giradot .... Mr. Abernathie
Lucien Littlefield .... Mr. Peters
Bodil Rosing .... Mrs. Klienschmidt
Herman Bing .... Mr. Kleinschmidt
Harry C. Bradley .... Mr. Warren
James B. Leonig .... Ram Singh
Shirley Temple .... Shirley Shaw
Lillian Harmer .... Louisa Mae Harrington
Torben Meyer .... Van Brinker

Story by Paul Harvey Fox
Screenplay by Austin Parker and Charles Kenyon
Directed by Michael Curtiz

NEW DEAL RHYTHM

Paramount

This was a two-reel musical featurette, with Shirley in a bit part. It served as her screen test for Paramount's purchased story, "Little Miss Marker"—or at least so said Paramount, possibly suggesting that after initially rejecting Shirley for *Marker*, this featurette made them reconsider.

Charles "Buddy" Rogers
Marjorie Main
Shirley Temple

(Opposite) A publicity pose for Change of Heart *shows Shirley with Janet Gaynor in* The World Is Ours, *the film's British title.*

CHANGE OF HEART

Fox Film Corp.; production #151

Two couples get confused as to who loves whom. One girl deserts her friends for a rich man, but she eventually realizes her mistake. Shirley's bit as one of the orphans was part of indoor shooting, which did not commence until outdoor scenes were completed. These took much longer than scheduled, resulting in Shirley's being kept at Fox until after she was to appear at Paramount to begin work on *Little Miss Marker*. Therefore, pre-production preparation, including wardrobe fittings, for *Marker* had to be abbreviated.

Janet Gaynor	Catherine Furness
Charles Farrell	Chris Thring
James Dunn	Mack McGowan
Ginger Rogers	Madge Rountree
Beryl Mercer	Harriet Hawkins
Gustav Von Seyffertitz	Mr. Krautzmann
Shirley Temple	Shirley
Irene Franklin	Greta Hailstrom
Fiske O'Hara	T. P. McGowan
Kenneth Thomson	Howard Jackson
Nella Walker	Mrs. Mockby
Barbara Barondess	Phyllis Carmichael

Based on the story "Manhattan Love Song," by Kathleen Norris
Screenplay by Sonja Levienen and James Gleason
Directed by John G. Blystone

BOTTOMS UP

Fox Film Corp

It is difficult to determine precisely when this film was made. In the October 1934 *Screenland*, Mrs. Temple wrote that Shirley's bit parts in *Bottoms Up* and *Change of Heart* came after *Stand Up and Cheer*. Possibly she meant that they were filmed after the rest of the film had been shot—or perhaps after the first song-and-dance sequence but before added Shirley footage had been shot. Whatever the case, the films were evidently released before Shirley's scenes were completed, since she got no billing notice.

Bottoms Up introduced British star Pat Paterson to American audiences. When not singing and dancing, she gets involved with gangsters.

Spencer Tracy	Smoothie King
John Boles	Hal Reede
Pat Paterson	Wanda Gale
Herbert Mundin	Limey Brock
Sid Silvers	Spud Mosco
Harry Green	Louis Wolf
Thelma Todd	Judith Marlowe
Robert Emmett O'Connor	Detective Rooney
Dell Henderson	Lane Worthing
Suzanne Kaaren	secretary
Douglas Wood	Baldwin

Story by B. G. DeSylva, David Butler, and Sid Silvers
Directed by David Butler

(Opposite) The still number indicates that this is a publicity shot, probably for the film Bottoms Up, *with Spencer Tracy. Fox may have dug out some buried photos once Shirley began to increase in popularity.*

STAND UP AND CHEER

Fox Film Corp.; May 1934; production #138

A Secretary of Amusement is appointed to the President's Cabinet to cheer on people with entertainment acts throughout the country to combat the Depression. The film was first titled *Fox Follies*, presumably when it consisted of follies acts and little if any storyline to link them.

In the film, the players appearing as themselves, plus some group acts, performed separate musical numbers, all of which were very loosely strung together. They were mostly brassy and pushy, so it is no wonder that Shirley's three scenes stood out with sweetness, charm, and WOW. Most memorable were her scenes with Dunn getting an interview; the performance with him of "Baby, Take a Bow," where Shirley emerges from gaudy chorus girls; and the closing sequence leading the band. The film also saw big-league football player Nick Foran changing jobs; he soon emerged as western star Dick Foran.

Warner Baxter .... Lawrence Cronwell, Secretary of Amusement
Madge Evans .... Mary Adams
Shirley Temple .... Shirley Dugan
James Dunn .... Jimmy Dugan, her father
Sylvia Froos .... as herself
John Boles .... as himself
Arthur Byron .... John Harley
Ralph Morgan .... secretary to the President
Aunt Jemima (Tess Gardell) .... as herself
Mitchell & Durant .... senators
Nick Foran .... as himself
Nigel Bruce .... Dinwiddie
"Skins" Miller .... hillbilly
Stepin Fetchit .... as himself

Story idea by Will Rogers and Philip Klein
Screenplay by Lew Brown and Ralph Spence
Songs by Lew Brown and Jay Gorney
Costumes by Rita Kaufman
Associate producer, collaborator on story and dialogue: Lew Brown
Directed by Hamilton McFadden
Produced by Winfield Sheehan

Jimmy Dunn introduces Shirley with the song "Baby, Take a Bow."

When Jimmy grabbed Shirley up to his side, there was instant rapport between them as well as with the audience.

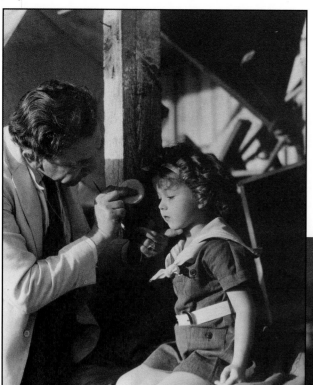

Here, Shirley's makeup is set for the closing sequence, in which she leads one of the bands of the parade.

Madge Evans, once a child star herself, was cast as head of the children's division for entertainment. But in Pic (October 15, 1940), it was claimed that this was Shirley's screen test for the film. Nothing else supports the claim, however. All other accounts have her auditioning with a song and dance.

Fox did a lot of publicity with Shirley starting with her Stand Up and Cheer *role—or, more correctly, when she began to draw attention. Here, she gets an autograph from dance director Sammy Lee. That looks like Gower Champion seated just beyond the piano's edge.*

LITTLE MISS MARKER

Paramount; June 1934; production #1491

Shirley is left by her father as a marker—that is, as security for a gambling loan. He loses and takes his own life, leaving Shirley to be claimed by Adolphe Menjou, owner of the gambling establishment. He works to make her a real home, helped by singer Dorothy Dell.

Initially, this film was titled *Half-Way Decent*; the British title was *Girl in Pawn*. However titled, it assured the Ideal Toy and Novelty Company that Shirley would be big enough to warrant a namesake doll, and it rushed the product onto the market in time for the Christmas season.

Adolphe Menjou .... Sorrowful Jones
Dorothy Dell .... Bangles Carson
Charles Bickford .... Big Steve
Shirley Temple .... Miss Marker (Martha, Marky)
Lynne Overman .... Regret
Frank McGlynn, Sr. .... Doc Chesley
Jack Sheehan .... Sun Rise
Gary Owen .... Grinder
Sleep 'n Eat .... Dizzy Memphis
Puggy White .... Eddie
Sam Hardy .... Benny the Gouge
Tammany Young .... Buggs
Edward Earle .... Marky's father
John Kelly .... Sore Toe
Warren Hymer .... Canvas-Back
Frank Conroy .... Dr. Ingalls
James Burke .... Reardon
Mildred Gover .... Sarah
Lucille Ward .... Mrs. Walsh
Crawford Kent .... doctor
Nora Cecil .... head of Home Finding Society

Based on a story by Damon Runyon, published in *Collier's*, 1932
Directed by Alexander Hall
Produced by B.P. Schulberg

An orphaned Shirley is taken to the Home Finding Society, but Dorothy and Adolphe want to give her a home. This still carries the original production number from Half-Way Decent. *The scene was dropped from* Marker *along with some other footage. Starting over, the film was renamed and renumbered.*

This British still shows Dorothy Dell and Shirley entering for the King Arthur party. It carries the British title and certificate of the film censor. Costume designer Edith Head was nominated for an Oscar for Shirley's Round Table outfit worn here.

Suave Adolphe Menjou was charmed by Shirley in Little Miss Marker. Little dolls need safety pins more than diamonds, but this was only a publicity pose.

The cover of "Laugh You Son-of-a-Gun"—which showed Dorothy Dell singing and a ragged little Shirley enchanted—was among the first sheet music to honor Shirley with her name and picture, making it especially sought after by collectors. By way of contrast, the first sheet music from Stand Up and Cheer just listed the performers' names. Later, special "Shirley covers" were issued for some of the songs.

Spencer Tracy was a New York gangster in Now I'll Tell. *Shirley is his rightly dubious daughter. On the other knee is Ronnie Crosbey.*

NOW I'LL TELL

Fox Film Corp.; made in April or May, released in July 1934.

A New York gangster risks his wife's love and his own life by his criminal activity. It was the same plot as Tracy's *Dante's Inferno*, but this was based on a true story.

Spencer Tracy	Murray Golden
Helen Twelvetrees	Virginia
Alice Faye	Peggy
Robert Gleckler	Mositer
Henry O'Nell	Doran
Hobart Cavanaugh	Freddie
G. P. Huntly, Jr.	Hart
Shirley Temple	Mary Golden
Ronnie Crosbey	Tommy, Jr.
Ray Cooke	Traylor
Frank Marlowe	Curtis
Clarence Wilson	Davis
Barbara Weeks	Wynne
Theodore Newton	Joe
Vince Barnett	Peppo
Jim Donlan	Honey Smith

Adapted from Mrs. Arnold Rothstein's *When New York Sleeps*,
a book based on the life of her gangster husband
Directed by Edwin Burke

A happy Shirley now sits on daddy Spencer's knee, watched by Barbara Weeks and Ronnie in the arms of Theodore Newton.

Director Harry Lachman plots the entire day's shooting of Baby, Take a Bow *on the board. Here come some last-minute changes. Actor Ray Walker watches. Behind them is script clerk Stanley Scheur.*

(Opposite) One scene at the top of the board is this one in which Shirley cuts the rope that her daddy, Jimmy, tied around Trigger, played by Ralph Harolde.

BABY, TAKE A BOW

Fox Film Corp.; summer 1934; production #158

Shirley's gangster father, Jimmy Dunn, released from prison, tries to go straight. A detective is trying to put him away once more, and an old gangster is trying to get him back to his old job. Unfortunately, Shirley befriends both detective and gangster, but there's a delightful party scene before the gun battle and final happy ending.

The film, initially called *Always Honest*, was made to take advantage of Shirley's "Baby, Take a Bow" song-and-dance routine in *Stand Up and Cheer*. To be sure everyone made the connection, the film was retitled. There was some controversy over *Stand Up and Cheer*'s gangster sequences, including one that found Shirley in the middle of the gunfight. Since the plot had already been used in several silent films, it was considered safe to use here—and a sure bet with Shirley.

Shirley Temple	Shirley Ellison
James Dunn	Eddie Ellison
Claire Trevor	Kay Ellison
Alan Dinehart	Welch
Ray Walker	Larry Scott
Dorothy Libaire	Jane
Ralph Harolde	Trigger Stone
James Flavin	Flannigan
Richard Tucker	Mr. Carson
Olive Tell	Mrs. Carson
John Alexander	rag picker

Story by Philip Klein and E. E. Paramore, Jr.
Directed by Harry Lachman
Produced by John Stone

Jimmy Dunn was the criminal determined to go straight because of his little girl. Shirley posed for several of these valentine photos during Baby, Take a Bow.

Shirley posed in all sorts of ways in this ballet dress. Assorted props were used, but this plain white circle displays her just fine.

(Opposite) Shirley adores her birthday ballet dress, but her mother, played by Claire Trevor, is worrying whether her husband will be sent back to jail.

NOW AND FOREVER

Paramount; released September 1934; production #1503.

Gary Cooper had deserted his little girl, played by Shirley, for a life of crime. He and girlfriend Toni, played by Carole Lombard, visit Shirley and he decides to straighten out his life—in the revised ending.

Before settling on *Now and Forever*, the film was called both *You Belong to Me* and *Honor Bright*. The latter was used for film publicity as a slogan for a children's truth-telling club, complete with pledge card. This helped to balance complaints against another gangster film featuring Shirley. The public considered Shirley such a draw for children that they also wanted stories to be suitable. Originally shot with a gun death for Gary and a suicide by Carole, in the sneak previews the public vehemently protested the ending. A new one was filmed featuring their reformation, the result of Shirley's influence.

Gary Cooper	Jerry Day
Carole Lombard	Toni Carstairs
Shirley Temple	Pennie (Penelope Day)
Sir Guy Standing	Felix Evans
Dog Buster	daschund
Charlotte Granville	Mrs. J. H. P. Crane
Gilbert Emery	James Higginson
Henry Kolker	Mr. Clark
Tetsu Komai	Mr. Ling
Andre Dheron	inspector
Jamison Thomas	Chris Carstairs
Harry Stubbs	Mr. O'Neill
Richard Lee	hotel clerk
Egon Brecher	doctor
Look Chan	assistant manager
Agostino Bergato	fisherman

Original story by Jack Kirkland and Melville Baker
Music and lyrics by Harry Revel and Mack Gordon
Directed by Henry Hathaway

(Opposite) A "story change" detailing a new ending for Now and Forever *was pasted into pressbooks. The original tragic conclusion had Gary and Carole bid farewell to Shirley, who was to be adopted, and then drive to an overlook where they could watch her train leave. Unbeknownst to Carole, Gary had been wounded in a gun battle, and he slumped over the wheel dead. In tears, Carole kissed him, then forced the car to an insane speed until it hurtled off the road into a ravine below.*

IMPORTANT STORY CHANGE

"Now and Forever"

Following first previews of "Now and Forever," reviewers, exhibitors and Paramount executives, tremendously impressed with the power of the story and the force of the sympathetic performances turned in by Gary Cooper, Carole Lombard, Shirley Temple and the whole cast, agreed unanimously that the picture merited and should logically conclude in a happy ending. Before release of "Now and Forever," changes were made in the closing reels. The revised synopsis below replaces the synopsis presented in the regular Press Book.

REVISED SYNOPSIS

not for publication

WITH money cleverly defrauded from a Chinese hotel chain, Jerry Day pays his overdue bill at the hotel, a member of the same chain, and debarks for the United States, where he hopes to extract $75,000 from his aristocratic brother-in-law, James Higginson, in return for full custody of Jerry's little daughter, Pennie.

Pennie's mother is long dead, and Jerry's traveling companion, beautiful Toni Carstairs, matches him in recklessness, shrewdness and adventurous spirit, but balks at the idea of selling his own child—even for $75,000. They separate.

Jerry meets Pennie and finds her a beautiful, spirited and imginative child, who is held down by the stultifying atmosphere of the Higginson home. He changes his mind, and takes her with him. The pair, father and tiny daughter, have a grand time "seeing New York" — riding Fifth Avenue buses, playing at Coney Island, shopping and eating—until Pennie falls sick from too much good time. They leave New York for Paris with funds Jerry obtains by selling a fictitious gold mine to Felix Evans.

Separation has convinced both Toni and Jerry that they cannot live apart. Toni welcomes him with open arms and extracts a promise from him that he will reform for the child's sake.

Jerry becomes a struggling real-estate salesman, sincere in his intention to go straight. Then he meets Evans again. The latter discloses himself as a jewel thief, and admits he purposely permitted Jerry to defraud him in New York so that he could force Jerry to become his accomplice. At first Jerry staunchly refuses to enter into any alliance.

A WEALTHY, elderly widow, Mrs. Crane, falls in love with Pennie, and offers to adopt her. She invites Jerry to bring her down to her home for a children's party before the child is sent away to school. Jerry's expenses outrun his salary, and, during the party at Mrs. Crane's home, he yields again to temptation and steals Mrs. Crane's necklace.

After a hectic search for the necklace fails, Pennie finds it concealed in her teddy bear, and is grief-stricken because she knows her father is a thief. She conceals her knowledge, however, until Jerry has given the necklace to Evans. When Toni discovers what is worrying the child, she pretends that it is she who has stolen it.

Ashamed, Jerry determines to set things right. He goes to Evans for the necklace but is forced to use a gun to get it. Evans is killed and Jerry is severely wounded. Concealing his injury, Jerry makes a full confession to Mrs. Crane and asks her to adopt Pennie.

Jerry and Toni bid a touching farewell to Pennie at the station from which she is leaving for school in the care of Mrs. Crane. Then Jerry faints from his wound after begging Toni not to take him to a doctor. When he comes to, he is in a doctor's office and Toni is bending over him explaining that she could not let him go on alone. Although both realized he will be punished, they resolve to face it together, and Toni assures the worried Jerry that Pennie will come to understand.

(Above) The pressbook also offered theaters an advertising herald to give away, a set of deluxe 11"x 14" photos to display in the lobby plus other items. This is just one page of the pressbook.

(Opposite) The window card went into display boxes all over town, these boxes being affixed to the sides of buildings, especially at alley entrances. The film ad filled about 8 ½" x 11" of space, which left another three inches at the top for the theater's name and play dates.

GARY
COOPER
CAROLE
LOMBARD
SHIRLEY
TEMPLE

in

NOW
AND FOREVER

a
Paramount
Picture

Presented by ADOLPH ZUKOR

Gary Cooper, who plays Shirley's daddy, is a gangster who has stolen a pearl necklace. The necklace is hidden inside Shirley's Grumpy bear.

(Opposite, top) Daddy Gary seems very happy to see his little girl, Pennie, played by Shirley. Charlotte Granville, who wishes to adopt Shirley, is concerned, and so is Gary's girlfriend, Carole.

(Opposite, bottom) Shirley plays happily with her Grumpy bear, unaware that Daddy Gary's keen interest is due to the pearl necklace he has hidden inside. Girlfriend Carole plays the piano but is uneasy, realizing something isn't quite right.

Prior to the filming of Bright Eyes, *Shirley was photographed in one of her movie outfits. She is wearing tap shoes, though as a little aviatrix she wouldn't need them in the film.*

BRIGHT EYES

Fox Film Corp.; December 1934; production #184.

When Shirley's mother is killed, there is a fight to determine who gains custody: the flyer friend of her dead father or some of the rich family for whom her mother had worked. The family's daughter-brat, played by Jane Withers, opposes the latter.

In this film about flyers, Shirley sang the song that became her theme, "On the Good Ship Lollipop." The fact that the Lollipop is an airship, not a boat, has been frequently ignored.

Shirley Temple .... Shirley Blake
James Dunn .... Loop Merritt, flyer
Jane Darwell .... Mrs. Higgins
Judith Allen .... Adele Martin
Lois Wilson .... Mary Blake, mother
Charles Sellon .... Uncle Ned Smith
Walter Johnson .... Thomas
Jane Withers .... Joy Smythe
Theodore Von Eltz .... J. Wellington Smythe
Dorothy Christy .... Anita Smythe
Brandon Hurst .... Higgins
George Irving .... Judge Thompson
David O'Brien .... flyer friend

Story by David Butler and Edwin Burke
Screenplay by William Conselman
Photography by Arthur Miller
Music by Richard A. Whiting and Sidney Clark
Numbers staged by Sammy Lee
Gowns by Royer
Directed by David Butler

Shirley and Jane Withers play dress-up while Jane's Uncle Ned (Charles Sellon) plays checkers with his film niece, Judith Allen. Sellon's big scene in Bright Eyes *is coming down the stairs in his wheelchair.*

Bright Eyes, *which included some holiday scenes, was planned for a Christmas 1934 release. Here, Shirley cuddles her rag doll while telling her mother, played by Lois Wilson, what she wants Santa to bring.*

A Christmas Day scene has flyer friends of Shirley's deceased father giving her a party and a ride in an airplane as it taxis around the field. In return, she sings what became her theme song, "On the Good Ship Lollipop."

THE LITTLE COLONEL

Fox Film Corp.; released February 1935; production #192.

A Southern colonel's daughter marries a Yankee against his will. When the colonel's daughter returns in poverty to occupy a small house she owns, there is war and peace brokered by her daughter, "Little Colonel" Shirley.

A Technicolor sequence of a "Pink Party" closed the film. The book on which the movie was based had been expanded into a popular series of stories, and the Alexander Doll Company secured a license from the owners of the book rights to create an actual "Little Colonel" doll to accompany the film's release. The Alexander doll would rival Ideal's "Shirley Temple" doll, which was dressed in a Little Colonel costume. Makers of games and children's clothes followed Alexander's lead.

Shirley Temple .... Lloyd Sherman, the Little Colonel
Lionel Barrymore.. Colonel Lloyd
Evelyn Venable .... Elizabeth Lloyd Sherman
John Lodge .... Jack Sherman
Sidney Blackmer.. Swazey
Alden Chase .... Hull
William Burress... Dr. Scott
David O'Brien ....Frank Randolph
Hattie McDaniel .... Mom Beck
Geneva Williams .... Maria
Avonne Jackson .... May Lily
Nyanza Potts .... Henry Clay
Frank Darien .... Nebler
Bill Robinson .... Walker

Based on the classic children's book by Annie Fellows Johnson
Screenplay by William Conselman
Directed by David Butler
Produced by B.G. De Sylva

A special Exploitation pressbook for The Little Colonel *urged people to make scrapbooks of Shirley Temple pictures and for merchants to tie-up. People of all ages saved the pictures. One thing was on target: those scrapbooks are valued treasures today.*

Tucked bodice, voile ruffles, fabric roses, soft curls: with all that pretty stuff there was no need to smile. The Little Colonel *dazzled.*

Shirley
TEMPLE
Lionel
BARRYMORE
in The
Little Colonel

with
EVELYN VENABLE
JOHN LODGE
BILL ROBINSON

A B. G. DeSYLVA PRODUCTION

FOX

In her Colonel *outfit, Shirley imitates Napoleon rather than the big Colonel, Lionel Barrymore. Even her eyes carry the pretense.*

(Opposite) This Little Colonel *window card was posted about town to announce the film's arrival. It is so gorgeous that one would expect most of the cards to have been swiped. After a very long and distinguished career, it must have been galling for Lionel Barrymore to have his name placed below that of Shirley.*

The Little Colonel *included some lovely costumes for Shirley, such as this petal frock. The antique chair is also wonderful.*

When Shirley goes to stay at the Colonel's mansion, aide Bill Robinson shows her a stair dance to get happily up to bed. This dance was his trademark. In some areas, people objected to the pair holding hands, and bits of the scene were cut.

Shirley and Bill repeated the dance steps for a sequence of publicity poses, this time with her in a bustle outfit.

Shirley and two plantation children imitate a baptism they have attended with Hattie McDaniel and Bill Robinson. It took a huge stack of sheets before the scene was finished just right.

The final scenes of The Little Colonel *showed a "Pink Party" filmed in Technicolor. Grandfather Lionel Barrymore frowns and Shirley poses with proper stiffness. Evelyn Venable and John Lodge know it is no longer a conflict of wills between them.*

(Opposite, top) Shirley came from a scene of playing in the mud to welcome a group of Japanese ship's officers. Only one seems glad to be there. They are not wearing prop weapons.

(Opposite, bottom left and right) These two snaps taken from a television showing of The Little Colonel *in Holland indicate that, rather than dubbing, the dialogue was given in Dutch subtitles. Facial expressions such as these are never caught in still poses.*

OUR LITTLE GIRL

Fox Film Corp.; released May 1935; production #201.

A busy doctor neglects his wife, and she begins to find interests elsewhere. They are about to break up, so their little girl feels unwanted and runs away. The parents' concern and love for their daughter reunite them.

Shirley Temple .... Molly Middleton
Rosemary Ames .... Elsa Middleton
Joel McCrea .... Dr. Donald Middleton
Lyle Talbot .... Rolfe Brent
Erin O'Brien-Moore .... Sarah Boynton
Poodles Hanneford .... as himself, circus clown
Margaret Armstrong .... Amy
Rita Owin .... Alice
Leonard Carey .... Jackson
J. Farrell MacDonald .... Mr. Tramp
The Hanneford Clowns .... as themselves
Dog .... Sniff
Jack Baxley .... Leyton

Based on the story "Heaven's Gate," by Florence Leighton Pfalzgraf
Screenplay by Stephen Avery, Allen Rivkin, and Jack Yellen
Directed by John Robertson
Produced by Edward Butcher

Outdoor scenes for Our Little Girl *included this one at Sherwood Lake. The original story called this spot Heaven's Gate, which was also the film's first title. Shirley's family reunites here at a favorite picnic area, and Shirley takes a picture.*

(Opposite)) In Our Little Girl, *doctor-daddy Joel McCrea comes home with gifts for Rosemary Ames and daughter Shirley, but this isn't enough to keep the family together.*

CURLY TOP

Fox Film Corp.; released July1935; production #216.

Shirley and her older sister, played by Rochelle Hudson, are orphaned. To the orphanage, they bring along their musical talents and Shirley's pony, all of which displeases some of the staff. Shirley and Rochelle are rescued by one trustee, played by John Boles, who adopts Shirley and marries her sister.

Although this was the first of a series of films based on books that were drastically altered as vehicles for Shirley, it still stands as having given her the most versatile role in her career. She sang and danced in Temple style, mimicked a crotchety old man, acted out a song sequence going from sweet sixteen to a young bride, and finally played an old lady with cracking voice. She also posed as Blue Boy and other characters from famous paintings.

Shirley Temple .... Elizabeth Blair (Betsy)
John Boles .... Edward Morgan, orphanage trustee
Rochelle Hudson .... Mary Blair, Betsy's sister
Jane Darwell .... Mrs. Denham
Rafaela Ottiano .... Mrs. Higgins
Esther Dale .... Aunt Genevieve
Arthur Treacher .... Morgan's butler
Etienne Girardot .... orphanage trustee
Maurice Murphy
Pony Spunky and duck .... Shirley's own

Based on the book *Daddy Long Legs*, by Jean Webster
Story adapted by William Conselman
Screenplay by Patterson McNutt and Arthur Beckhard
Music by Ray Henderson
Lyrics by Ted Koehler, Edward Heyman, and Irving Caesar
Directed by Irving Cummings
Produced by Winfield Sheehan

(Opposite, top) Again an orphan in Curly Top, Shirley mimicks an old, stern trustee in his overcoat. Orphanage head Rafaela Ottiano is upset with Shirley, as is trustee Etienne Girardot. Staffer Jane Darwell is upset with his scolding Shirley, while trustee John Boles enjoys it all.

(Opposite, bottom) Wealthy John Boles is so happy with Shirley that he adopts her, while her sister, played by Rochelle Hudson, becomes his love interest.

In his study, the wealthy John Boles daydreams and sees his famous paintings come to life as poses of Shirley. Here it is "The Helping Hand," by Émile Renouf. Siegfried Rumann is the fisherman.

(Opposite, top) Shirley sang a specialty number, "When I Grow Up," that started with herself, presumably, as a six-year-old. Next comes this sixteen-year-old ready to party. Shirley gets some unique hairstyling and some discreetly added bodice-padding.

(Opposite, bottom) In the song, Shirley progresses to becoming a bride at twenty-one.

The "When I Grow Up" song ends with Shirley as an old woman of sixty-five rocking in her chair and singing in a cracking voice.

THE LITTLEST REBEL

Twentieth Century-Fox; released January 1936; production #236.

Shirley plays a Southern child, sheltered and indulged, until the war tears her family and world apart. She learns to accept help from the hated enemy Yankee and gains both safety and a friend.

Shirley Temple	Virginia Houston Cary (Virgie)
John Boles	Confederate Captain Herbert Cary
Jack Holt	Union Colonel Morrison
Karen Morley	Mrs. Cary
Bill Robinson	Uncle Billy, Cary servant
Guinn Williams	Sergeant Dudley
Willie Best	James Henry
Frank McGlynn, Sr.	President Lincoln
Bessie Lyle	Mammy
Hanna Washington	Sally Ann

Based on the book *The Littlest Rebel*, by Edward Peple
Screenplay by Edwin Burke and Harry Tugend
Directed by David Butler
Associate producer: B.G. De Sylva
Produced by Darryl F. Zanuck

Rebel Captain Herbert Cary (John Boles) is Shirley's father in The Littlest Rebel. *Here, he succeeds in convincing her to be brave as he prepares to leave for the battlefront.*

Shirley's birthday party minuet scene is interrupted by news of war, and the mothers hurry to snatch children from the dancing to rush them home. Shirley wants to keep her partner, Freddie McManus.

(Opposite, top) Shirley puts on shoe black and a kerchief to disguise herself from marauding Yankees. Director David Butler had to get a shot for his own album.

(Opposite, bottom) In her blackface scene, Yankee Guinn Williams snatches off her bandana and pushes her mother down the stairs. Rebel Shirley protests with hair-pulling and a fist.

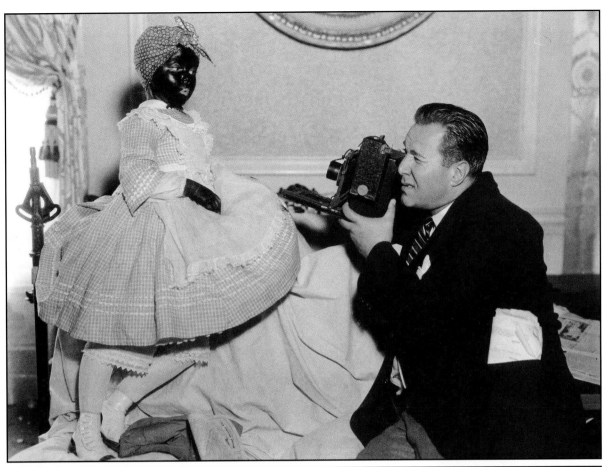

A typical outdoor shot for The Littlest Rebel *involves a complicated setup of reflectors, overhead speakers, and camera. Director Butler has his back to the viewers of this scene. Shirley has shut her eyes to rest them.*

(Opposite) For the scene of Shirley visiting prisoner Jack Holt, everything is a fake setup, which with careful cropping will look totally convincing.

See Shirley Temple Birthday Section

movie MIRROR

MAY 1936

10¢

A MACFADDEN PUBLICATION

SHIRLEY TEMPLE

By May 1936 The Littlest Rebel *was still in wide circulation, and* Movie Mirror *used this color photo of star Shirley in her lovely party frock to grace its cover. It appears that one of her front teeth is a temporary replacement. Inside, the magazine had a special feature honoring Shirley's April birthday.*

(Opposite) A sober Shirley—complete with birthday party hairdo, frock, and hand-held hanky—posed for still photos.

CAPTAIN JANUARY

Twentieth Century-Fox; released April 1936; production #242.

Orphaned Shirley is saved from a shipwreck by a lighthouse keeper. A truant officer insists on better surroundings and schooling, but relatives are finally found to rescue everyone.

In the film, besides performing a difficult dance sequence on circular stairs, Shirley joins Guy Kibbee and Slim Summerville in an operatic trio that combines comedy with some excellent timing and pretty fair vocalizing.

Shirley Temple	Star
Guy Kibbee	Captain January
June Lang	Mary Marshal
Slim Summerville	Captain Nazro
Buddy Ebsen	Paul Rogers
Sara Haden	Agatha Morgan
Jane Darwell	Eliza Croft
Jerry Tucker	Cyril Morgan
Nella Walker	Mrs. John Mason
George Irving	John Mason
James Farley	Deputy Sheriff
Si Jenks	old sailor
John Carradine	East Indian
Mary McLaren	nurse at aunt's home
Billy Benedict	messenger boy

Based on the book *Captain January*, by Laura E. Richards
Screenplay by Sam Hellman, Gladys Lehman, and Harry Tugend
Music by Lew Pollack, Sidney D. Mitchell, and Jack Yellen
Dances staged by Jack Donohue
Photographed by John Seitz
Costumes by Gwen Wakeling
Settings by Thomas Little
Associate producer: B.G. De Sylva
Directed by David Butler
Produced by Darryl F. Zanuck

(Opposite) The Captain January *window card came with a blank top space to list theater and play dates.*

The 22" x 28" theater lobby card, shown here much reduced, was posted behind glass in the theater entry to entice viewers.

(Opposite) The nicest theater advertising was the 14" X 36" insert card posted at the lobby entrance. The large Shirley photo got every patron into a happy mood.

(Right) Shirley's dance partner in Captain January was Buddy Ebsen. Their lengthy "At the Codfish Ball" routine took them over kegs, boxes, barrels, and flooring on the new Will Rogers soundstage. Settings are by Thomas Little.

(Below) As the orphan Star in Captain January, Shirley got a frock cut down from her opera-singer mother's trunkful of effects. This was a good excuse for Slim Summerville and Guy Kibbee to join her in an operatic trio that was almost too good for the comedy they put into it.

THE POOR LITTLE RICH GIRL

Twentieth Century-Fox; released July 1936; production #257.

Shirley's rich father is too busy to spend time with her. She gets lost, becomes a radio star with some new friends, and this leads to just the advertising her father needs for his soap company. The film was mere Temple formula until the closing military dance sequence, which was outstanding.

Shirley Temple	Barbara Barry
Alice Faye	Jerry Dolan
Gloria Stuart	Margaret Allen
Jack Haley	Jimmy Dolan
Michael Whalen	Richard Barry, Barbara's father
Sara Haden	Collins
Jane Darwell	Woodward
Claude Gillingwater	Simon Peck
Henry Armetta	Tony
Arthur Hoyt	Percival Gooch
John Wray	Flagin
Paul Stanton	George Hathaway
Charles Coleman	Stebbins
John Kelly	Ferguson
Tyler Brooks	Dan Ward
Mathilde Comont	Tony's wife
Leonard Kilbrick	Freckles
Dick Webster	soloist
Bill Ray	announcer
Gayne Whitman	announcer (assumed)

Based on the book *The Poor Little Rich Girl*, by Eleanor Gates
Story adapted by Eleanor Gates and Ralph Spence
Screenplay by Sam Hellman, Gladys Lehman, and Harry Tugend
Associate producer: B.G. De Sylva
Directed by Irving Cummings
Produced by Darryl F. Zanuck

In The Poor Little Rich Girl, *Michael Whalen was Shirley's doting single parent when he wasn't busy with his own affairs. This was a publicity photo, and a real departure from Shirley's usual smile or pout poses.*

When Shirley's governess is struck by a car while escorting her to a train, self-reliant Shirley takes off on her own, joining street children and then the family of organ grinder Henry Armetta.

A behind-the-scenes view of a boom—a glorified crane atop which the cameraman perches to get this shot of "poor little rich girl" Shirley joining Alice Faye and Jack Haley for a song-and-dance scene. In her autobiography, Child Star, Shirley tells how hard the trio later worked to synchronize their taps to the filmed sequence, a much more difficult task than dubbing dialogue or songs for sound recording.

British publicity for The Poor Little Rich Girl *included this Christmas cover on* Picture Show *(December 26, 1936), and also a special film souvenir inside.*

(Opposite) This Poor Little Rich Girl *window card announced the film's prevue on Saturday night at 11:15, when adults would be able to enjoy Shirley without a bunch of noisy kiddies in the audience.*

TIVOLI Theatre

PREVUE
SAT. NITE
11:15

SUNDAY - - MONDAY - - TUESDAY
WEDNESDAY ❋ JULY 19-22

Shirley TEMPLE in THE POOR LITTLE RICH GIRL

DIRECTED BY
IRVING CUMMINGS
ASSOCIATE PRODUCER
B. G. DeSYLVA
SUGGESTED BY THE STORIES BY
ELEANOR GATES AND RALPH SPENCE

20th CENTURY FOX

ALICE FAYE   GLORIA STUART
JACK HALEY   MICHAEL WHALEN

SARA HADEN JANE DARWELL
CLAUDE GILLINGWATER

A FOX PICTURE
DARRYL F. ZANUCK
IN CHARGE OF PRODUCTION

DIMPLES

Twentieth Century-Fox; production #268.

Grandfather, played by Frank Morgan, is not providing the proper atmosphere for Dimples, and a rich lady seeks to adopt the child—Shirley. But Dimples needs love more than atmosphere.

Dimples was first called *The Bowery Princess*, but with Shirley in the movie, crowds objected to the connotation. In the film she went from ragged boyish clothes to period frocks, and there was the brief staging of scenes from the play *Uncle Tom's Cabin*, including Shirley as the dying Little Eva. Temple fans cried at Shirley's affecting portrayal; critics complained that Shirley looked too healthy to be dying.

Shirley Temple	Sylvia Dolores Appleby (Dimples)
Frank Morgan	Professor Appleby, her grandfather
Helen Westley	Mrs. Caroline Drew
Robert Kent	Allen Drew
Delma Byron	Betty Loring
Astrid Allwyn	Cleo Marsh
Stepin Fetchit	Cicero
Berton Churchill	Colonel Loring
Paul Stanton	Mr. St. Clair
Julius Tannen	Hawkins
John Carradine	Richards
Herman Bing	proprietor
Billy McClain	Rufus
The Hall Johnson Choir	choir
Jack Clifford	Uncle Tom
Betty Jean Hainey	Topsy
Arthur Aylesworth	pawnbroker
Greta Meyer	proprietor's wife
Leonard Kilbrick, Warner Weidler, Walter Weidler, George Weidler	children's band
Jesse Scott and Thurman Black	the Two Black Dots

Screenplay by Arthur Sheekman and Nat Perrin
Dances staged by Bill Robinson
Music by Jimmy McHugh and Ted Koehler
Photography by Bert Glennon
Costumes by Gwen Wakeling
Assistant director: Booth McCracken
Associate producer: Nunnally Johnson
Directed by William A. Seiter
Produced by Darryl F. Zanuck

(Opposite) The Dimples *window card shows Shirley scolding her grandfather and also in the pink tuxedo finale costume.*

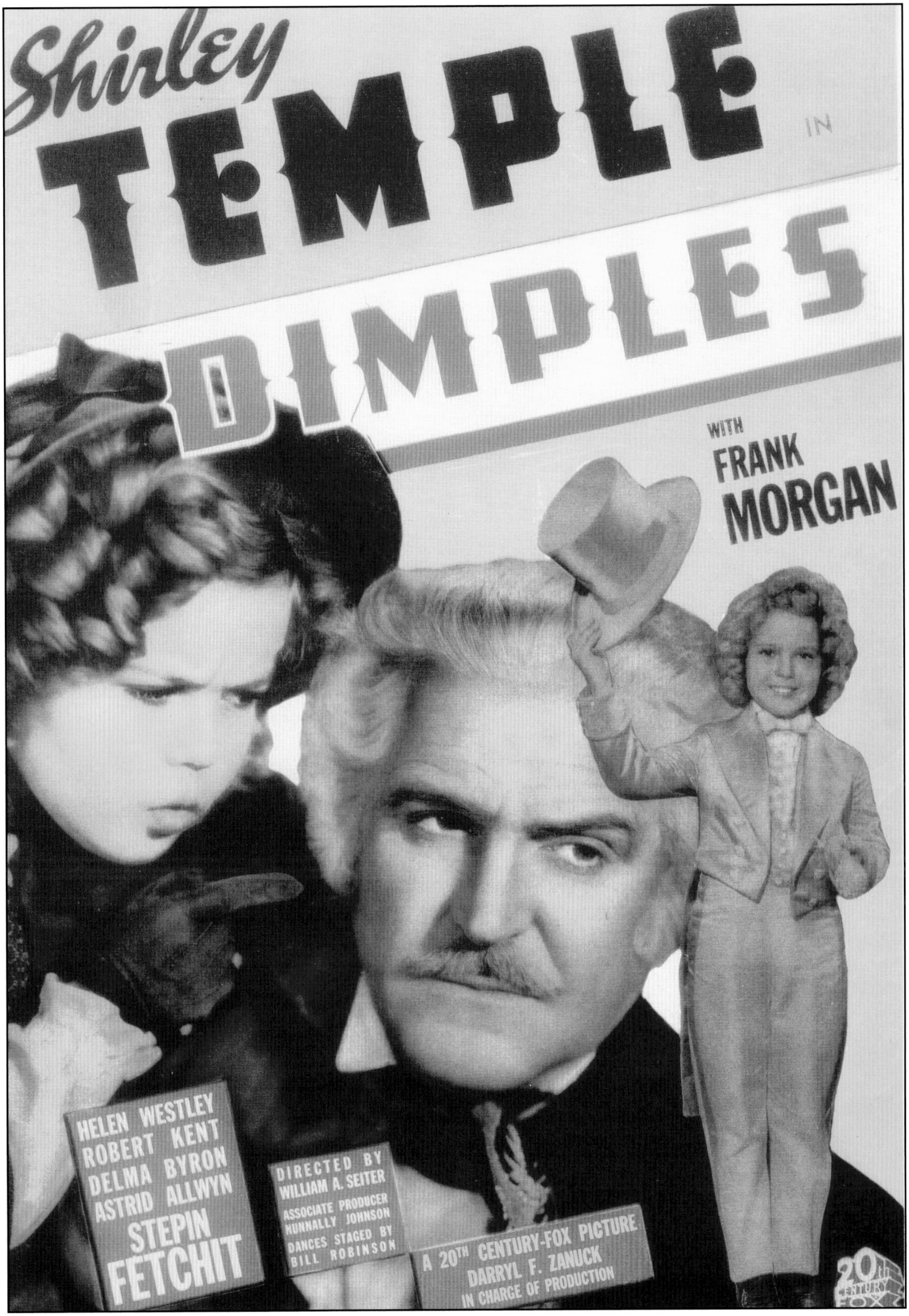
Shirley
TEMPLE
IN
DIMPLES
WITH
FRANK
MORGAN
HELEN WESTLEY
ROBERT KENT
DELMA BYRON
ASTRID ALLWYN
STEPIN
FETCHIT
DIRECTED BY
WILLIAM A. SEITER
ASSOCIATE PRODUCER
NUNNALLY JOHNSON
DANCES STAGED BY
BILL ROBINSON
A 20TH CENTURY-FOX PICTURE
DARRYL F. ZANUCK
IN CHARGE OF PRODUCTION
20th CENTURY FOX

This Dimples *publicity pose of Shirley with Frank Morgan contrasts his precise coiffure with a capped Shirley.*

(Opposite, top) Intimate scenes were often anything but that in reality. Here, under the hot lights and watchful eyes of director William Seiter and photographer Bert Glennon, Shirley pleads with her grandfather in a cold, drafty tenement setting.

(Opposite, bottom) When Shirley plays Little Eva to Frank Morgan, who is seen here in blackface as Uncle Tom in the play Uncle Tom's Cabin, *her hair seems to have lost a great deal of its volume.*

Wearing her pink satin tuxedo for the finale, Shirley is carried from her portable dressing room on the back of assistant director Booth McCracken. Here, she has loads of hair.

In Mickey's Polo Team, a Walt Disney cartoon (1936), Shirley was among the fans of Mickey's team—namely, the Three Little Pigs.

STOWAWAY

Twentieth Century-Fox; December 1936; production #289.

The orphaned daughter of missionaries in China befriends a playboy in need of a translator. Due to confusion, Shirley unwittingly ends up as a stowaway on the ship on which he is traveling. In the film, Shirley imitates Ginger Rogers and Fred Astaire in a dance scene, plus the singing of Al Jolson and Eddie Cantor.

The cast also included Shirley's Pekingese dog, Ching-Ching, a gift from Doc Bishop. Audiences might have wondered once more who would take time to fix an orphan's hair with all those Shirley curls. The film first announced that she would have braids, but that was considered too daring. A publicity photo also showed Helen Westley spanking Shirley, but that also was abandoned.

Shirley Temple .... Ching-Ching, daughter of missionaries
Robert Young .... Tommy Randall
Alice Faye .... Susan Parker
Eugene Pallette .... the Colonel
Helen Westley .... Mrs. Hope
Arthur Treacher .... Atkins
J. Edward Bromberg .... Judge Booth
Astrid Allwyn .... Kay Swift
Allan Lane .... Richard Hope
Robert Greig .... Captain
Jayne Regan .... Dora Day
Julius Tannen .... First Mate
Willie Fung .... Chang
Philip Ahn .... Sun Lo
Paul McVey .... Second Mate
Helen Jerome Eddy .... Mrs. Kruikshank
William Stack .... Alfred Kruikshank
Honorable Wu .... Latchee Lee

Story by Sam Engel
Screenplay by William Conselman, Arthur Sheekman, and Nat Perrin
Photography by Arthur Miller
Costumes by Royer
Music by Mack Gordon, Harry Revel, and Irving Caesar
Associate producers: B.G. De Sylva, Earl Carroll, and Harold Wilson
Directed by William A. Seiter
Produced by Darryl F. Zanuck

A Famous Christmas Painting in Full Color

"The Adoration of the Magi" — Reproduced in Today's Issue — See Pages 10 and 11

SUNDAY MIRROR

PAGES OF COMICS 16

5¢ PAY NO MORE

New York, N. Y. **MAGAZINE SECTION** SUNDAY DECEMBER 20, 1936

SHIRLEY TEMPLE

Photographed in Natural Color in Hollywood Especially for the Sunday Mirror Magazine. (See Page 18.)

Many of Shirley's movie costumes were designed by Gwen Wakeling. However, the Stowaway *credits list Royer. Here, Shirley's personal dressmaker, Elise Deal, is fitting the collar. Once a costume was just right, duplicates were made using Shirley's special dress form.*

(Opposite) Stowaway *was planned as a Christmas season release, and publicity included this* New York Sunday Mirror *cover of December 20, 1936.*

"Stowaway" Shirley peeks at her three teachers from inside her portable dressing room. Nearest Shirley is regular teacher Frances Klamt, but to help Shirley learn some four hundred Chinese words for this film, Bessie Nyi was secured. A recent addition to the staff was French teacher Paula Walling. The three are also sharing a special book of Chinese papercuts.

Shirley's costars in Stowaway are lovely Alice Faye, heading to the Orient to marry her fiancé, and rich playboy Robert Young, who changes Alice's mind with Shirley's help.

WEE WILLIE WINKIE

Twentieth Century-Fox; released July 1937; production #307.

While visiting her Colonel grandfather in India, Shirley befriends a prisoner who is the leader of rebel natives. When they attack the British compound, Shirley goes to beg for peace.

Shirley claimed that this was her favorite film and the kilt her favorite outfit. Publicity did credit her with adding several bits of business that gave touches of realism. The film, shot in sepia tone, opened first as a roadshow attraction of 105 minutes, which was too long for ordinary release and was therefore cut. Again Shirley was briefly naughty and properly spanked, though there was no acknowledgment that her character's fraternizing with the prisoner, duped though she was, helped him escape the rebel attack.

Shirley Temple .... Priscilla Williams (Winkie)
Victor McLaglen .... Sergeant MacDuff
C. Aubrey Smith .... Colonel Williams
June Lang... Joyce Williams, Shirley's mother
Michael Whalen .... Lieutenant Brandes, called Coppy
Cesar Romero .... Khoda Khan, rebel leader
Constance Collier .... Mrs. Allardyce
Douglas Scott .... Private Mott
Gavin Muir .... Captain Bibberbeigh
Willie Fung .... Mohammet Dihu
Brandon Hurst .... Bagby
Lionel Pape .... Major Allardyce
Clyde Cook .... Pipe Major Sneath
Lauri Beatty .... Elsie Allardyce
Lionel Braham .... Major General Hammond
Mary Forbes .... Mrs. MacMonachie
Cyril McLaglen .... Corporal Tummel
Pat Somerset .... officer
Hector Sarno .... driver
Jack Pennick .... soldier guard and Shirley's military instructor offstage

Story by Rudyard Kipling
Screenplay by Ernest Pascal and Julien Josephson
Associate producer: Gene Markey
Directed by John Ford
Produced by Darryl F. Zanuck

In Wee Willie Winkie, *Shirley's grandfather (the Colonel), played by C. Aubrey Smith, seems a heartless tyrant and she protests his authority—to his shock and the barely concealed amazement of Sergeant MacDuff, played by Victor McLaglen. Brandon Hurst as Bagby, the Colonel's aide, keeps stiff upper eyelids.*

(Opposite) Jack Pennick carefully tutored Shirley in military matters, then took his part in the film as a guard. As such, here he ignores Shirley.

Sergeant MacDuff helps Private Winkie aim her miniature rifle.

When Sergeant MacDuff is dying from wounds brought on by the natives, Shirley brings him stolen flowers and sings "Auld Lang Syne." Then Shirley and the audience cried their eyes out.

HEIDI

Twentieth Century-Fox; released in late November 1937 for the Christmas season; production #322.

Orphaned Shirley as Heidi is dumped on her grandfather, high in the Alps, much to his displeasure. Then her aunt decides that Shirley can be profitable and returns to snatch her away. Heidi is taken to Frankfurt to serve as playmate to rich invalid Klara. The aunt is paid and leaves. The grandfather comes seeking Heidi, who runs away to find him. They are reunited and, with Heidi's help, Klara learns to walk.

One of the problems of preparing a film for Christmas release was the absence of snow in the California summer. The snow scenes were shot under canvas on a hot day. Moth crystals were the snow, and the smell was worse than the heat. The studio provided two wigs for Shirley, one as Marie Antoinette in a court dance scene; the other was a version of braids first planned for *Stowaway*.

Shirley Temple .... Heidi
Jean Hersholt .... Adolph Kramer, grandfather
Arthur Treacher .... Andrews
Helen Westley .... Blind Anna
Pauline Moore .... Elsa
Thomas Beck .... Pastor Schultz
Mary Nash .... Fraulein Rottenmeier
Sidney Blackmer .... Herr Sesemann
Mady Christians .... Aunt Dete
Sig Rumann .... police captain
Marcia Mae Jones .... Klara Sesemann
Delmar Watson .... Peter, the goat boy
Egon Brecher .... innkeeper
Christian Rub .... baker
George Mumbert .... organ grinder

Based on the book *Heidi*, by Johanna Spyri
Screenplay by Walter Ferris and Julien Josephson
Directed by Allan Dwan
Produced by Darryl F. Zanuck

In Heidi, Jean Hersholt was a stern grandfather to Shirley, but they were good friends walking on the studio back lot.

As Heidi, Shirley dreamed of happy scenes from a storybook. She awakens to do a clever Dutch wooden shoe dance that was copied in many public school programs. For the film, Shirley got entirely new hair, not just a new hairdo.

Heidi's dreaming continued to let Shirley be Marie Antoinette and descend the stairs for this stately minuet.

In the rear seat of a sleigh, Marcia Mae Jones, Shirley, and Sidney Blackmer seem to be enjoying a wonderful winter scene. Alas, the time was summer; the set was covered over to get the right lighting; the snow was just moth crystals that smelled awful. Yet they look so happy!

(Opposite) The Heidi *window card is very nice art, but somehow it doesn't quite capture the real Shirley.*

REBECCA OF SUNNYBROOK FARM

Twentieth Century-Fox; released fall 1938; production #343.

Shirley, unwanted as unproductive by her stepfather and his new wife, is taken to live on her aunt's farm. When she sings on the radio, he recognizes her voice and earning potential and takes her back. But the aunt and Shirley, who want to stay together, win in the end.

The "Toy Trumpet" song by Raymond Scott was originally announced as having lyrics written by Shirley at his request—but that was just publicity. Actually, others wrote the words and Shirley sang them rapidly to the staccato music.

Better known from *Rebecca* is the sequence beginning "I'd like to reminisce." That became the theme of Shirley Temple film festivals in the 1950s, which reintroduced child Shirley to a new audience on television. The superpushy stepfather was probably too mild a representation of stage parents. Candy manufacturers were up in arms over Aunt Miranda's criticism of a candy bar as not being a decent meal. There was something for everyone to love or hate.

Shirley Temple .... Rebecca Winstead
Randolph Scott .... Anthony Kent
Jack Haley .... Orville Smithers
Gloria Stuart .... Gwenn Warren, Shirley's cousin
Phyllis Brooks .... Lola Lee
Helen Westley .... Aunt Miranda Wilkins
Slim Summerville .... Homer Busby
Bill Robinson .... Aloysius
Raymond Scott Quintet .... as themselves
Alan Dinehart .... Purvis
J. Edward Bromberg .... Dr. Hill
Dixie Dunbar .... receptionist
Paul Hurst .... Mug
William Demarest .... Henry Kipper, the stepfather
Ruth Gillette .... Melba
Paul Harvey .... Cyrus Bartlett
Clarence Hummel Wilson .... Jake Singer
Sam Hayes, Gary Breckner, Carroll Nye .... radio announcers
Franklin Pangborn .... Hamilton Montmarcy

Based on the classic book by Kate Douglas Wiggin,
but so altered as to bear little resemblance to the original.
Screenplay by Karl Tunberg and Don Ettlinger
Cinematography by Arthur Miller
Costumes by Gwen Wakeling
Dances staged by Nick Castle and Geneva Sawyer
Music by Lew Pollack, Mack Gordon, Harry Revel, Sidney D. Mitchell, Sam Pokrass, Jack Yellen, Raymond Scott
Associate producer: Raymond Griffith
Directed by Allan Dwan
Produced by Darryl F. Zanuck

Cousins Rebecca (Shirley) and Gwenn (Gloria) get acquainted on the farm, and Shirley shares her problems. This is a specially tinted photo for theater display.

Shirley and Bill Robinson are doing a soft-shoe routine at Sunnybrook Farm. They dropped metal blackberries into the buckets to add flavor to the sounds of their feet.

Everyone tries to convince Aunt Miranda to let Rebecca sing on the radio. There are Randolph Scott and Shirley, Slim Summerville, and Gloria Stuart. So Helen Westley agrees.

While Shirley poses in her "Toy Trumpet" outfit for the director and staff, there is one unidentified man who is not at all interested in the Rebecca star.

LITTLE MISS BROADWAY

Twentieth Century-Fox; production #362.

Orphaned Shirley is taken by family friends to live in a hotel for theatrical performers. A rich neighbor objects to their lowbrow noise and tries to evict them all. A courtroom demonstration of their talents serves as evidence of their worth and the neighbor relents.

Again, this was a formula film, but Shirley continued to wear the new hairdo that had been introduced in *Rebecca*, with the famous curls pulled to the side. Shirley was even shown with her curls pinned close to the head for the night, though it had always been claimed that the curls were natural.

Early publicity for *Little Miss Broadway* showed Shirley doing a current dance, called the "Big Apple" in captions. The more recent discovery and showing of vault film that had been cut has identified this as part of the interchange and dance with Jimmy Durante.

Shirley Temple	Betsy Brown
George Murphy	Roger Wendling
Jimmy Durante	Jimmy Clayton
Phyllis Brooks	Barbara Shea
Edna May Oliver	Sarah Wendling
George Barbier	Fiske
Edward Ellis	Pop Shea
Jane Darwell	Miss Hutchins
El Brendel	Ole
Donald Meek	Willoughby Wendling
Patricia Wilder	Flossie
Claude Gillingwater, Sr.	judge
George and Olive Brasno	as themselves
Charles Williams	Mike Brody
Charles Coleman	Simmons
Russell Hicks	Perry
Brian Sisters	as themselves for a specialty number
Brewster Twins	guests
Claire DuBrey	Miss Blodgett
Robert Gleckler	detective
C. Montague Shaw	Miles
Frank Dae	Pool
Eddie Collins, Syd Saylor, Jerry Colonna, Heinie Conklin	members of the band
Clarence Hummel Wilson	Scully
Ben Weldon	taxi driver

Original screenplay by Harry Tugend and Jack Yellen
Dances staged by Nick Castle and Geneva Sawyer
Photography by Arthur Miller
Music by Walter Bullock and Harold Spina
Costumes by Gwen Wakeling
Associate producer: David Hempstead
Directed by Irving Cummings
Produced by Darryl F. Zanuck

In Little Miss Broadway, *Shirley is again in an orphanage. Soon to be adopted, she joins fellow singers (played by the Brian Sisters) in a farewell song, "Be Optimistic."*

At home in the Shea Hotel for performers, Shirley is put to bed by Phyllis Brooks as Barbara Shea. Shirley's curls were carefully pinned, as in her everyday fashion. Fans got a more realistic glimpse of the normal Shirley in this scene.

The climax of Little Miss Broadway *had Shirley as that character dancing with suave George Murphy. They made their way down Broadway and across rooftops of the New York skyline, complete with flashing lights—all as part of a courtroom exhibit.*

By the time Little Miss Broadway *was released, this scene with Jimmy Durante had been cut. This footage, released from studio vaults, identifies the dance and song as "Hop, Skip, Jump and Slide."*

JUST AROUND THE CORNER

Twentieth Century-Fox; production #372.

Shirley's widowed father is the maintenance man at a hotel, while his former fiancée lives in the penthouse with Shirley's uncle, the building owner. Shirley helps her father get a better job and reunites the pair with considerable mischief.

Again, Shirley's dog, Ching-Ching, had a part in the film, which was initially called *Lucky Penny*. The studio did less publicity for this film, but it was also issuing fewer films. There were only seven films between *Little Miss Broadway* and *Just Around the Corner*.

Corner was considered another stock film with assorted character types to contrast with Shirley. Some reviewers objected strongly. Perhaps these films should simply have been presented as a series of Shirley Temple adventures, similar to the Bobbsey Twins or Nancy Drew.

Shirley Temple	Penny Hale
Charles Farrell	Jeff Hale
Joan Davis	Kitty
Amanda Duff	Lola
Bill Robinson	Corporal Jones, doorman
Bert Lahr	Gus
Franklin Pangborn	Waters, hotel manager
Cora Witherspoon	Aunt Julia Ramsby
Claude Gillingwater, Sr.	Samuel G. Henshaw
Bennie Bartlett	Milton Ramsby
Hal K. Dawson	reporter
Charles Williams	candid cameraman
Eddie Conrad	French tutor
Tony Hughes and Orville Caldwell	Henshaw's assistants
Marilyn Knowlden	Gwendolyn

Based on an original story by Paul Gerard Smith
Screenplay by Ethel Hill, J.P. McEvoy, and Darrell Ware
Songs by Walter Bullock and Harold Spina
Dances staged by Nicholas Castle and Geneva Sawyer
Photographed by Arthur Miller
Costumes by Gwen Wakeling
Associate producer: David Hempstead
Directed by Irving Cummings
Produced by Darryl F. Zanuck

After a job failure, Charles Farrell as Shirley's father takes a job as the hotel maintenance man. Shirley keeps house in their basement apartment.

One of Shirley's musical numbers lets her join with hotel employees Bert Lahr, Joan Davis, and Bill Robinson.

Shirley cut the curls from penthouse dweller Bennie Bartlett, and he acquired less sissyish clothes in a fight. Shirley helps him explain to his distraught mother and grouchy grandfather. This Just Around the Corner *lineup includes Cora Witherspoon, Claude Gillingwater, Sr., and Franklin Pangborn.*

Shirley
TEMPLE
in
JUST AROUND
THE CORNER
with
Charles
FARRELL
Joan
DAVIS · DUFF
Amanda
BERT LAHR
BILL ROBINSON
Franklin
PANGBORN · WITHERSPOON
Cora
Bennie
BARTLETT
DARRYL F. ZANUCK
in charge of production
Directed by IRVING CUMMINGS
CENTURY-FOX PICTURE

THE LITTLE PRINCESS

Twentieth Century-Fox; production #399.

Shirley's widowed father indulges her in a princess lifestyle, but he goes to war in South Africa and is reported dead. The matron of Shirley's boarding school then demotes her former prize-income resident to an attic bed and servant's work. Shirley searches for her father, finds him in a hospital, and brings happiness to nearly everyone, including fellow servant Sybil Jason.

Listed as Diedre Gale in the cast was Diedre Gale Broughton, who had won a contest in Great Britain as a Shirley Temple lookalike. She was brought to Hollywood to meet Shirley, as many others were, but her chief prize was this movie role. Shirley left her throne in a dream sequence to perform a simple ballet. More convincing was a real-life cockney song-and-dance routine with the marvelous Arthur Treacher. But, as always, there were some cruel elders to mistreat her.

Shirley Temple	Sara Crewe
Richard Greene	Geoffrey Hamilton
Anita Louise	Rose
Ian Hunter	Captain Crewe
Cesar Romero	Ram Dass
Arthur Treacher	Bertie Minchin
Mary Nash	Amanda Minchin
Sybil Jason	Becky
Miles Mander	Lord Wickham
Marcia Mae Jones	Lavinia
Beryl Mercer	Queen Victoria
Deidre Gale	Jessie
Ira Stevens	Ermengarde
E. E. Clive	Mr. Barrows
Eily-Malyon	cook
Clyde Cook	attendant
Keith Kenneth	Bobbie
Will Stanton and Harry Allen	grooms
Holmes Herbert, Evan Thomas, Guy Bellis	doctors
Kenneth Hunter	general
Lionel Braham	colonel

Based on the book by Frances Hodgson Burnett
Screenplay by Ethel Hill and Walter Ferris
Associate producer: Gene Markey
Directed by Walter Lang
Produced by Darryl F. Zanuck

(Opposite) The Corner window card emphasized Shirley, music, comedy, and love.

A special portrait for The Little Princess *shows a graceful and not-so-little relaxed young lady.*

(Opposite) Long before the concept of "good vibes," Shirley and Arthur Treacher shared a special dance greeting in The Little Princess, *where she boards among snobby rich girls and he helps his sister run the school.*

Though her father is reported dead, Shirley insists that he is alive and keeps hunting till she finally finds him in the hospital with amnesia and ready to be shipped elsewhere.

In a dream sequence, Shirley imagines herself a real princess, complete with throne and courtiers in medieval style. Now, Arthur Treacher is her sidekick court jester.

SUSANNAH OF THE MOUNTIES

Twentieth Century-Fox; production #412.

The sole survivor of an Indian massacre, Shirley is rescued by the Royal Canadian Mounted Police. Then she helps them improve relations with the Indians and rescues her Mountie benefactor.

During the filming, Shirley became an honorary princess in the Blackfoot Indian tribe. The Indian Service permitted twelve chiefs to leave the reservation to appear in the film, with sizable bail posted against their proper care. Shirley studied some authentic Americana while Hollywood "Indians" complained about being left out. There was no cute Shirley Temple in the film, though she rode her own pony, Roanie, had several coy scenes, and an upset stomach after smoking a peace pipe.

Shirley Temple .... Susannah Sheldon
Randolph Scott .... Inspector Angus Montague, called Monty
Margaret Lockwood .... Vicky Standing
Martin Good Rider .... Little Chief
J. Farrell MacDonald .... Pat O'Hannegan
Maurice Moscovich .... Chief Big Eagle
Moroni Olsen .... Superintendent Andrew Standing
Victor Jory .... Wolf Pelt
Lester Matthews .... Harlan Chambers
Leyland Hodgson .... Randall
Herbert Evans.. doctor
Jack Luden .... Williams
Charles Irwin .... Sergeant McGregor
John Sutton.. Corporal Piggot
Chief Big Tree .... Chief

Based on the book *Susannah of the Mounties*, by Muriel Denison
Adapted by Fidel La Barba and Walter Ferris
Screenplay by Robert Ellis and Helen Logan
Directed by William A. Seiter
Produced by Darryl F. Zanuck

The Smart Screen Magazine

SCREENLAND

September

NOW
10¢

7d in England

SHIRLEY
TEMPLE

HOLLYWOOD
CHANGES
OVER-NIGHT!
SAYS
VICKI BAUM

HONEST CONFESSIONS OF AN EXTRA GIRL
Who's Who on Elsa Maxwell's Hollywood Party List

Mounties rescue Shirley as Susannah, sole survivor of the massacre. Randolph Scott is her protector as an Inspector in the Royal Canadian Mounted Police.

(Opposite) Susannah of the Mounties *let Shirley enjoy Native American culture and dress, as shown on the cover of the September 1939* Screenland.

Despite her bad experience, Shirley becomes a blood "brother" of Little Chief, played by Martin Good Rider, and finally brings peace.

Perhaps reminiscent of a similar scene in Little Miss Marker, Shirley kneels to pray in a back room of Mountie quarters, watched by J. Farrell MacDonald.

THE BLUE BIRD

Twentieth Century-Fox; production #442.

While searching for the Blue Bird of Happiness in exotic places, Shirley and her brother discover that it is to be found at home. The story was presented as written—a magical journey, not a dream.

This classic was rearranged so that Mytyl was older than her brother to give Shirley the role of leadership. Much to-do was made over finding a boy who looked enough like Shirley. In the film, Shirley was crabby and given little opportunity for childish song and dance, emphasizing the story more than the star. It was a lovely, meaningful film.

Though considered a bomb and omitted from early Temple television festivals, *The Blue Bird* has more recently been given good showings. The lack of big-money receipts at home did not repay film costs but, despite gathering war clouds overseas, it evidently earned enough to break even.

Shirley Temple .... Mytyl
Spring Byington .... Mummy Tyl
Nigel Bruce .... Mr. Luxury
Gale Sondergaard .... Tylette the cat
Eddie Collins .... Tylo the dog
Sybil Jason .... Angela Berlingot
Jessie Ralph .... Fairy Berylune
Helen Ericson .... Light
Johnny Russell .... Tyltyl
Laura Hope Crews .... Mrs. Luxury
Russell Hicks .... Daddy Tyl
Cecilia Loftus .... Granny Tyl
Al Shean .... Grandpa Tyl
Gene Reynolds .... studious boy
Leona Roberts .... Mrs. Berlingot
Stansey Andrews .... Wilheim
Dorothy Dearing .... Cypress
Frank Dawson .... Caller of Roll
Claire DuBrey .... nurse
Sterling Holloway .... Wild Plum
Thurston Hall .... Father Time
Edwin Maxwell .... Oak
Herbert Evans, Brandon Hurst .... footmen
Dewey Robinson .... Royal Forester
Keith Hitchcock .... Major Domo
Buster Phelps .... boy inventor
Tommy Taker, Dorothy Joyce .... lovers
Billy Cook .... boy chemist
Scotty Beckett, Juanita Quigley, Payne Johnson .... children
Ann Todd .... little sister
Diane Fisher .... little girl

Based on the story by Maurice Maeterlinck
Screenplay by Ernest Pascal
Associate producer: Gene Markey
Directed by Walter Lang
Produced by Darryl F. Zanuck

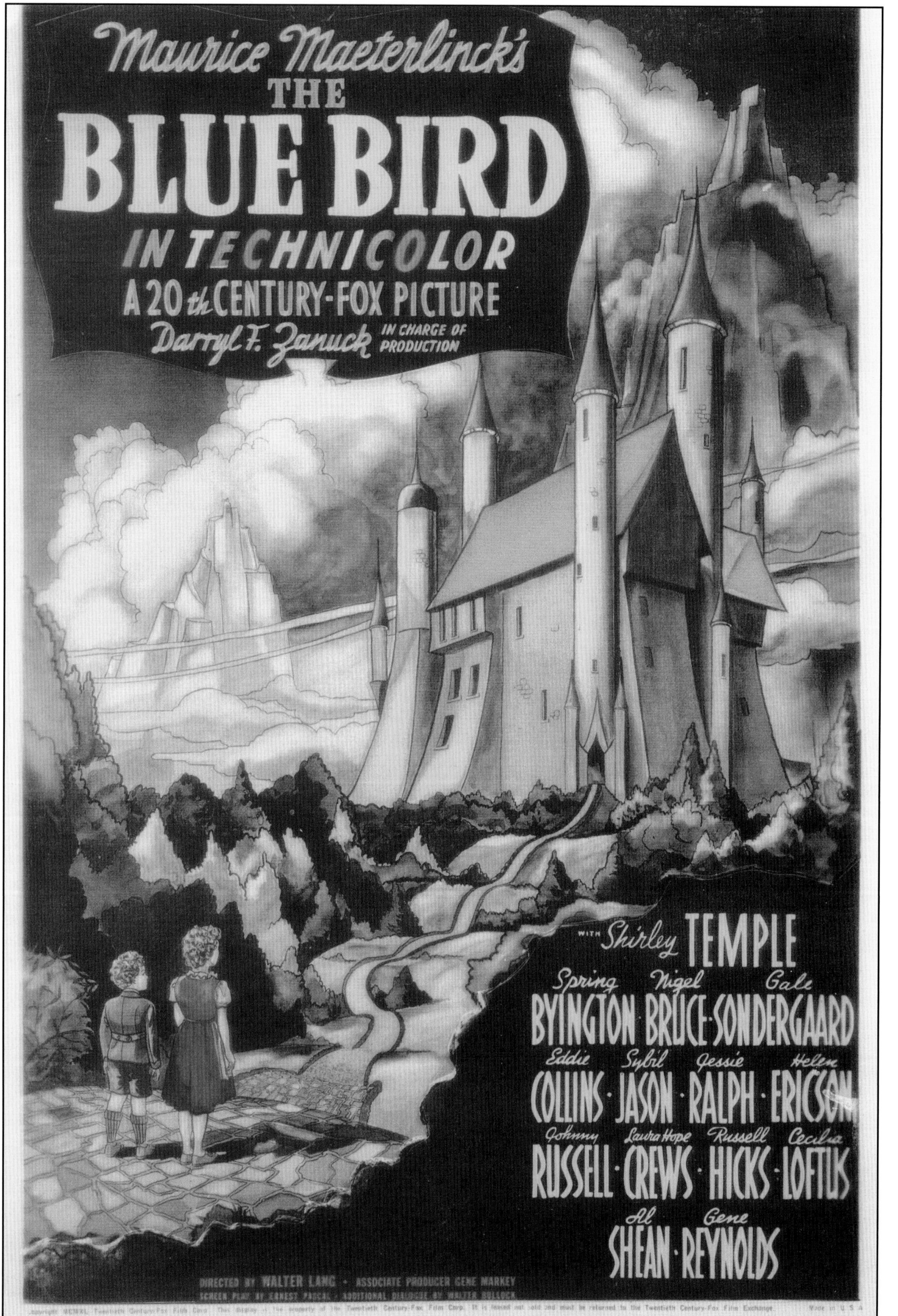
Maurice Maeterlinck's
THE BLUE BIRD
IN TECHNICOLOR
A 20th CENTURY-FOX PICTURE
Darryl F. Zanuck IN CHARGE OF PRODUCTION
WITH Shirley TEMPLE
Spring BYINGTON · Nigel BRUCE · Gale SONDERGAARD
Eddie COLLINS · Sybil JASON · Jessie RALPH · Helen ERICSON
Johnny RUSSELL · Laura Hope CREWS · Russell HICKS · Cecilia LOFTUS
Al SHEAN · Gene REYNOLDS
DIRECTED BY WALTER LANG · ASSOCIATE PRODUCER GENE MARKEY
SCREEN PLAY BY ERNEST PASCAL · ADDITIONAL DIALOGUE BY WALTER BULLOCK

A lobby card from The Blue Bird *shows the cemetery scene with Gale Sondergaard, Eddie Collins, Johnny Russell, and Shirley. It also has the censor stamp-of-approval (lower left corner) for overseas showing.*

(Opposite) The Blue Bird *window card was artistic, but more of a fantasy than the film itself.*

Sheet music from The Blue Bird *was published by Robbins Music Corp., not Fox, and sold in Canada.*

Shirley and her little brother, Johnny Russell, decide to hunt for the Blue Bird of Happiness and show invalid Sybil Jason their bird cage.

Hunting for the Blue Bird in the Land of Luxury, Shirley is pampered by Laura Hope Crews as Mrs. Luxury. Gale Sondergaard, as the cat, hopes Shirley will be kept from leaving.

YOUNG PEOPLE

Twentieth Century-Fox; production #467.

Shirley and her adoptive parents leave show business to settle on a farm. Their neighbors snub them until they rescue a group of children from a flood.

This return to the Temple formula of song-and-dance and mistreatment was Shirley's last before her parents bought up the remainder of her Twentieth Century-Fox contract. Charlotte Greenwood and Jack Oakie seemed to be playing themselves after long years of real vaudeville. A sequence of early Temple film clips was surely designed to pacify fans—and these were welcomed. But this was a weak film, well deserving its second-attraction status at most theaters.

Shirley Temple .... Wendy Ballantine
Jack Oakie .... Joe Ballantine
Charlotte Greenwood .... Kit Ballantine
Arleen Whelan .... Judith
George Montgomery .... Mike Shea
Kathleen Howard .... Hester Appleby
Minor Watson .... Dakin
Frank Swann .... Fred Willard
Frank Scully .... Jeb
Sara Edwards .... Mrs. Stinchfield
Mae Marsh .... Marie Liggett
Irving Bacon .... Otis
Charles Halton .... moderator
Arthur Aylesworth .... doorman
Olin Howland .... station master
Billy Wayne .... stage manager
Harry Tyler .... Dave
Darryl Hickman .... Tommy
Shirley Mills .... Mary Ann
Diane Fisher .... Susie
Bobby Anderson .... Jerry Dakin

Screenplay by Edwin Blum and Don Ettlinger
Directed by Allan Dwan
Produced by Harry Joe Brown

Arleen Whelan consoles the dejected Shirley after the town's young people snub her.

Shirley organizes a jazzy "Young People" revue the teens love but which horrifies the parents and further alienates her from the town's elders, who see to it that the youngsters follow suit.

In Young People, *orphaned Shirley joins vaudeville friends of her parents. After retiring to a farm, the three resurrect their act, hoping to entertain neighbors who prove unappreciative.*

KATHLEEN

Metro-Goldwyn-Mayer; production #1207.

Shirley, trying to preserve her privacy, drives a housekeeper up the wall. Her busy father hires a live-in psychologist to discover Shirley's problems. Counselor Laraine Day discovers that the motherless young teen is lonely, dislikes her father's fiancée, and just needs a real friend. Day moves from psychologist to friend to fiancée and all is well.

The film, originally titled *The Girl on the Hill*, was made after Shirley signed with MGM to do one film for a salary of $2,000 a week. Following the release of this film about typical teen insecurities and longings, Shirley was hailed as "The New Shirley Temple," who could act, was beautiful instead of cute, and had great promise.

Shirley Temple	Kathleen Davis
Herbert Marshall	John Davis, her father
Laraine Day	Dr. A. Martha Kent
Gail Patrick	Lorraine Bennett
Nella Walker	Mrs. Farrell
Felix Bressart	Mr. Schoner
Lloyd Corrigan	Dr. Montague Foster
Guy Bellis	Jarvis
Wade Boteler	policeman
Charles Judels	manager
Else Argal	maid
Margaret Bert	Margaret
Joe Yale	sign poster

Original story by Kay Van Riper
Screenplay by Mary C. McCall, Jr.
Directed by Harold S. Bucquet
Produced by George Haight

Psychologist Laraine Day is hired as a live-in counselor to determine Shirley's problem. The diagnosis is loneliness and neglect, so Day becomes a dependable friend.

Shirley surprises housekeeper Nella Walker peeking through the keyhole to her private room. She claims that Shirley has a problem.

In some theaters, Kathleen *had top billing. MGM gave it good publicity with these two 22" x 28" photo lobby cards.*

MISS ANNIE ROONEY

United Artists; production #E.S. 36300.

A jiving teenage Shirley accidentally meets a rich boy, played by Dickie Moore, whom she invites to a gathering. In turn, he invites her to his fancy party. Shirley's father crashes the party and demonstrates an invention, which explodes, causing a mess. Despite the fiasco, the demonstration leads to a job for her father with Moore's company, and Dickie becomes Shirley's hero.

In *Miss Annie Rooney*, Shirley got her first *real* screen kiss. Of course, this did not include the Baby Burlesks and others. But now she was older and this was a fourteen-year-old boy who provided the kiss, so it made big news.

Except for a horrible hat, Shirley's outfits in the film were really the authentic teen garb of the time—hep. Her hair had become amazingly straight after the frizzed look she had in *Young People* and even *Kathleen*. She just kept getting more lovely.

Shirley Temple .... Annie Rooney
William Gargan .... Tim Rooney, her father
Guy Kibbee .... Grandpop
Dickie Moore .... Marty
Peggy Ryan .... Myrtle
Roland DuPree .... Joey
Gloria Holden .... Mrs. White
Jonathan Hale .... Mr. White
Mary Field .... Mrs. Metz
George Lloyd .... Burns
Jan Buckingham .... Madam Sylvia
Selmer Jackson .... Mrs. Thomas
June Lockhart .... Stella Bainbridge
Charles Coleman .... Sidney
Edgar Dearing .... policeman
Virginia Sale .... Myrtle's Mother
Shirley Mills.. Audrey Hollis

Screenplay by George Bruce
Directed by Edwin L. Marin
Produced by Edward Small

Shirley's boyfriend, Joey, played by Roland DuPree, rear-ends the car of rich boy Dickie Moore, and he cannot take Shirley on to the teen party. So, Dickie offers to escort Shirley.

Shirley is all ready for rich Dickie's party, so Shirley, father William Gargan, and grandpop Guy Kibbee celebrate.

Shirley teaches Dickie to jitterbug at the party.

SINCE YOU WENT AWAY

United Artists; production #V.P.

Claudette Colbert's husband goes off to war, leaving her and their two daughters, Shirley Temple and Jennifer Jones, to cope. Financial problems necessitate their taking in a boarder, played by Monty Woolley. The realistic storyline includes the death of Monty's grandson, who is Jennifer's love.

This deeply moving war film, with its compassion and not-too-blatant patriotism, has been considered something of a classic. "Together," an old World War I song, was the background theme for Jennifer and her love, played by real-life but soon-to-be-estranged husband Robert Walker. The song beautifully expressed World War II feelings.

The film cast included three honorably discharged wounded veterans.

Shirley was part of a great team in this film, David Selznick's first production since *Gone With the Wind*, and she also witnessed his developing love for Jennifer. The film introduced Guy Madison, who went on to many bigger parts.

Claudette Colbert .... Anne Hilton
Jennifer Jones .... Jane
Shirley Temple .... Bridget (Brig)
Hattie McDaniel .... Fidelia
Jane Devlin .... Gladys Brown
Lloyd Corrigan .... Mr. Mahoney
Monty Woolley .... Colonel Smollet
Agnes Moorehead .... Emily Hawkins
Joseph Cotten .... Lieutenant Anthony Willett
Robert Walker .... Corporal William G. Smollet II
Jackie Moran .... Johnny Mahoney
Guy Madison .... Harold Smith, a sailor
Lionel Barrymore .... clergyman
Craig Stevens .... Danny Williams
Albert Wasserman .... Mr. Sigmund Gottlieb Golden
Nazimova .... Zofia Kislowska, a welder
Keenan Wynn .... Lieutenant Solomon

Based on the book by Margaret Buell Wilder
Screenplay by David O. Selznick
Directed by John Cromwell
Produced by David O. Selznick

Director John Cromwell joins stars Hattie McDaniel, Shirley Temple, and Claudette Colbert plus producer David O. Selznick as they discuss their film's success.

(Opposite, top) Jennifer Jones, Claudette Colbert, and Shirley Temple confidently plan to deal with wartime problems.

(Opposite, bottom) Robert Walker joins the family in taking their worries to church. Just behind them is an unsympathetic Agnes Moorehead.

I'LL BE SEEING YOU

United Artists; production #V.D.F. and V.D.F.-S.

Ginger Rogers, on Christmas leave from prison, meets Joseph Cotten, who is fighting battle shock. They fall in love, but there is more shock when her cousin, played by Shirley, reveals Ginger's prison background. Some ads listed this film as presented by Selznick International; others identified it as a David O. Selznick film.

Ginger Rogers .... Mary Marshall
Joseph Cotten .... Zachary Morgan
Shirley Temple .... Barbara Marshall, Mary's cousin
Spring Byington .... Mrs. Marshall
Tom Tully .... Mr. Marshall
Chill Wills .... Swanson
Dare Harris .... Lieutenant Bruce (Dare Harris was later renamed John Derek)
Kenny Bowers .... sailor on the train
Olin Howlin .... hawker
Dorothy Stone .... salesgirl
John James .... paratrooper
Eddie Hall .... Charlie Hartman
Joe Haworth .... sailor in coffee shop
Jack Carr .... counterman
Bob Meredith .... soldier-father on train
Robert Dudley .... YMCA hotel attendant
Margaret Bert .... mother of boys
Mickey Laughlin, Hank Tobias, Gary Gray .... boys
Earl W. Johnson .... dog owner

Story by Charles Martin
Screenplay by Marion Parsonnet
Directed by William Dieterle
Produced by Dore Schary

TAKE IT OR LEAVE IT

Twentieth Century-Fox.

Into this film based on the Phil Baker radio show and starring Baker himself, Fox inserted clips from a group of the studio's hits as one contestant's category. Among them was Shirley's "Baby, Take a Bow" sequence from *Stand Up and Cheer*. So, Shirley appeared in this film without credit or payment. That would happen many more times in later years.

A portrait of Shirley in her Christmas party gown in I'll Be Seeing You. *She wore the same gown celebrating her sixteenth birthday on the set in April 1944.*

Over Christmas, Ginger visits her aunt, Spring Byington, and meets Joseph Cotten. Shirley watches their interest spark.

KISS AND TELL

Columbia; production #C.D. 814.

Shirley's father is convinced that his daughter's best friend, Mildred, is leading her astray. Dad starts a feud with Mildred's entire family, unaware that Shirley's absent soldier-brother is secretly married to Mildred. Sworn to secrecy about the marriage, Shirley visits the obstetrician with Mildred, and everyone—to their horror—assumes that Shirley is pregnant and must be married off quickly. The soldier-son arrives home on leave just in the nick of time.

The film version of this top-ranking Broadway hit gave Shirley many dramatic and comedic opportunities, but part of the film's popularity was a result of the real-life publicity of Shirley's engagement and marriage to John Agar. A radio show, *Meet Corliss Archer*, was a spinoff of the film, but Shirley was not involved.

Shirley Temple	Corliss Archer
Jerome Courtland	Dexter Franklin
Walter Abel	Mr. Archer
Katherine Alexander	Mrs. Archer
Robert Benchley	Uncle George, a chaplain
Porter Hall	Mr. Franklin
Edna Holland	Mrs. Franklin
Virginia Welles	Mildred Pringle
Tom Tully	Mr. Pringle
Darryl Hickman	Raymond Pringle
Scott McKay	Private Jimmy Earhart
Scott Elliott	Lenny Archer

Based on the Broadway play by F. Hugh Herbert
Screenplay by F. Hugh Herbert
Directed by Richard Wallace
Produced by Sol C. Siegel

In Kiss and Tell, *Shirley is doing a poor job selling linens at a charity bazaar. She persuades boyfriend Jerome Courtland to make a purchase, rewarding him with a kiss. Suddenly she has a long line of customers— for kisses.*

In February 1945, Shirley accepted the Junior Critics award for Since You Went Away *on behalf of David O. Selznick.* Review, *the national broadcast, featured George Burns and Gracie Allen, so Shirley joined in the horseplay.*

Shirley won a debate with her mother and wore these white slacks to the studio. Wardrobe okayed them for the scene in Kiss and Tell, *adding the midriff effect.*

HONEYMOON

RKO; production #HIM.

Shirley and her soldier-fiancé meet in Mexico City to marry and honeymoon during his brief leave. Assorted legal and personal obstacles interfere. The film's romantic triangle and wedding made use of the continuing publicity surrounding Shirley's own wedding and experiences as a bride.

Honeymoon had a bit of foreign flavor, a song-and-dance to please old fans, but still a silly plot. The initial plan was to film in Mexico City, but that also presented obstacles, so lookalike locations were chosen.

Shirley Temple .... Barbara Olmstead
Franchot Tone .... David Flanner
Guy Madison .... Phil Vaughn, fiancé
Lina Romay .... Racquel Mendoza
Gene Lockhart .... Prescott
Corinna Mura .... Señora Mendoza
Grant Mitchell .... Crenshaw
Julio Vilareal .... Señor Mendoza
Manual Arvide .... registrar
Jose R. Goula .... Doctor Diego

Story by Vicki Baum
Screenplay by Michael Kanin
Directed by William Keighley
Produced by Warren Duff

Shirley is dunked in the pool during one of Honeymoon's *problems. New problem: where are the Temple natural curls?*

285

When Shirley and fiancé Guy Madison finally get together to be married, Tony Roux informs them that witnesses are required.

This isn't a dance. Shirley practices a judo throw with Guy Madison, but in the film she floors Franchot Tone.

THE BACHELOR
AND THE BOBBY-SOXER

RKO; production #BBS.

Shirley develops a teenage crush on playboy artist Cary Grant and hides out in his apartment. Shirley's sister, a judge played by Myrna Loy, sentences Grant to escort Shirley until the crush wears off. Cary does such a good job that Myrna abandons boyfriend Rudy Vallee in favor of him.

The first of two films in which she appeared with older men, in this one Cary Grant was finally given to Myrna Loy, and Shirley aged-down as a young teenager. Wardrobe seemed out of touch with regular teens at times, especially for this film, and many wrote protest letters to the studio and fan magazines objecting to such things as Shirley's heels with bobby-sox: totally oog! Cary Grant and Rudy Vallee gave excellent comedy competition. Producer Dore Schary stepped into the film to appear as Cary's best friend.

Cary Grant	Dick
Myrna Loy	Margaret
Shirley Temple	Susan
Rudy Vallee	Tommy
Ray Collins	Bemish
Harry Davenport	Uncle Thaddeus
Johnny Sands	Jerry
Don Beddoe	Tony
Lillian Randolph	Bessie
Veda Ann Borg	Prescott
Dan Tobin	Walters
Ransom Sherman	Judge Treadwell
William Bakewell	Winters
Irving Bacon	Melvin
Ian Bernard	Perry
Carol Hughes	Florence
William Hall	Anthony Herman
Gregory Gay	maître d'hôtel

Story by Sidney Sheldon
Screenplay by Sidney Sheldon
Directed by Irving Reis
Produced by Dore Schary

When Cary Grant gives a school art lecture, student Shirley Temple is mesmerized. Beside her, boyfriend Johnny Sands misses the magic.

At the big picnic, Shirley's hero is Cary Grant, who always loses. Winner Rudy Vallee gloats while Myrna Loy, Ray Collins, and Harry Davenport remain unimpressed.

THAT HAGEN GIRL

Warner Bros.-First National; production #683.

Town gossips question the legitimacy of Mary Hagen, played by Shirley, and they put her down at every turn. Things come to a head when Tom Bates, portrayed by Ronald Reagan, returns to town and is reputed to be her father. He isn't. Finally, in despair, Mary attempts suicide; he rescues her and they fall in love.

This second film in which Shirley was featured with an older man had Ronald Reagan as the love interest. This time Shirley was presented as more mature in attitude to bridge the age gap, but it was awkward at best. A much better plot was the *Romeo and Juliet* school play within the film, in which Shirley was a lovely young Juliet.

Shirley Temple	Mary Hagen
Ronald Reagan	Tom Bates
Dorothy Peterson	Minta Hagen, mother
Charles Kemper	Jim Hagen
Rory Calhoun	Ken Freneau
Jean Porter	Sharon Bailey
Nella Walker	Molly Freneau
Winifred Harris	Selma Delaney
Ruth Robinson	Cora
Lois Maxwell	Julia Kane
Conrad Janis	Mary's dance date, Dewey Koons
Penny Edwards	Christine Delaney
Harry Davenport	Judge Merrivale

Based on the novel by Edith Roberts
Screenplay by Charles Hoffman
Directed by Peter Godfrey
Produced by Alex Gottlieb

Scandalous gossip resulted in boyfriend Rory Calhoun's abandoning Shirley. At first Ronald Reagan was enmeshed in the same scandal. Then he became an understanding friend and . . . finally . . . they fell in love.

Much preparation went into the making of That Hagen Girl. Here, Shirley holds the ID board for the second of about five tests for hairstyle. There were similar makeup and costume tests.

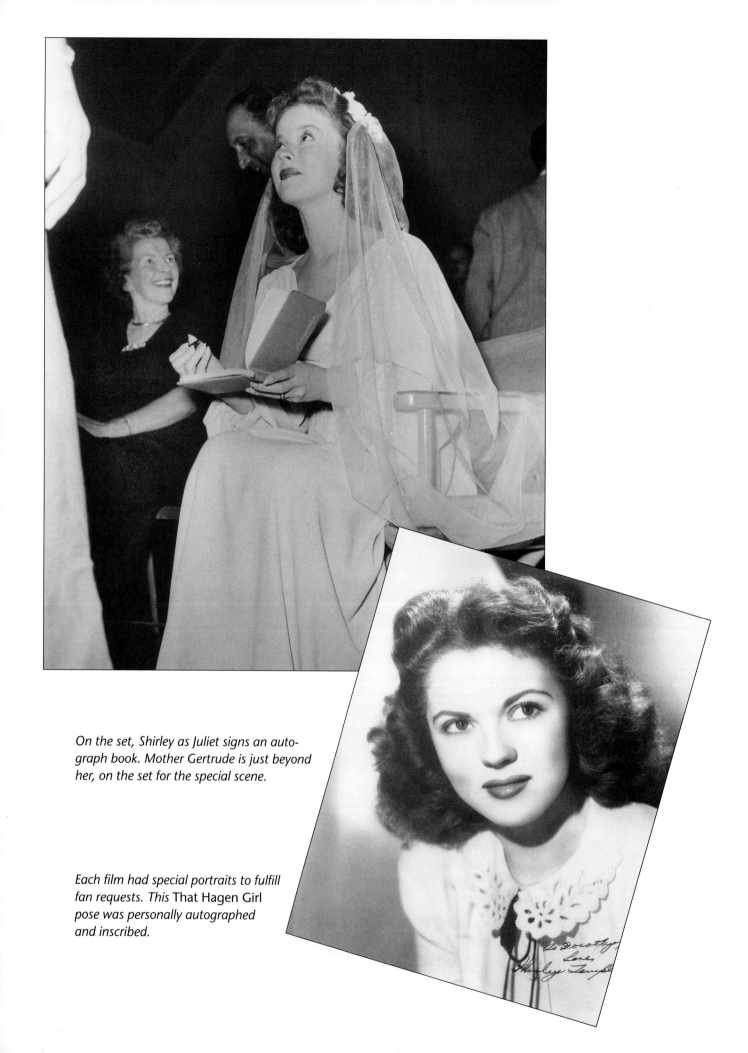

On the set, Shirley as Juliet signs an auto-graph book. Mother Gertrude is just beyond her, on the set for the special scene.

Each film had special portraits to fulfill fan requests. This That Hagen Girl *pose was personally autographed and inscribed.*

FORT APACHE

Argosy Pictures Production, RKO release; production #WP-P.

Henry Fonda is Shirley's colonel-father, determined to keep the Indians under control even if it kills him and a lot of Fort Apache's men. Wiser heads cannot change the impending massacre, though John Wayne tries. Shirley's boyfriend, a newly commissioned lieutenant, escapes to bring the sad news back to the fort.

This movie was a typical big western that did nothing for Shirley's career except to give her more big-name costars and the opportunity to introduce husband John Agar to the moviegoing public.

John Wayne	Captain York
Henry Fonda	Colonel Thursday
Shirley Temple	Philadelphia Thursday
Pedro Armendariz	Sergeant Beaufort
Ward Bond	Sergeant O'Rourke
George O'Brien	Captain Collingwood
John Agar	Lieutenant O'Rourke
Victor McLaglen	Sergeant Mulachy
Anna Lee	Mrs. Collingwood
Irene Rich	Mrs. O'Rourke
Miguel Inclan	Chief Cochise
Dick Foran	sergeant
Jack Pennick	sergeant
Guy Kibbee	post surgeon
Grant Withers	Indian agent
Mae Marsh	post resident

Story by James Warner Bellah, based on the story "Massacre,"
in *The Saturday Evening Post*
Screenplay by Frank S. Nugent
Directed by John Ford
Presented by John Ford and Merian C. Cooper

Along with John Wayne and John Agar, Shirley is a dinner guest of the Collingwoods, played by George O'Brien and Anna Lee, at Fort Apache.

Henry Fonda is a colonel with a mission: to be a medal-winning hero. He is already a tyrant to Ward Bond, Irene Rich, his daughter Shirley, and her boyfriend (in the film) John Agar.

Shirley and her mother, Josephine Hutchinson, favor "Votes for Women." Mob objection leads to their arrest.

ADVENTURE IN BALTIMORE

RKO; production #BES.

Independent Shirley crusades for women's suffrage and ends up in jail. She paints boyfriend John Agar bare to the waist and nearly gets her minister-father fired. Actually, Shirley wore so much makeup in the film that any pastor-father of 1905 would have been fired. The parades for women's votes were more realistic.

In *Adventure in Baltimore*, first a very hep modern teen Shirley appears briefly, and then the scene shifts to the past. First titles for the film were *Baltimore Escapade* and *Bachelor Bait*.

Robert Young	Dr. Sheldon, minister
Shirley Temple	Dinah Sheldon
John Agar	Tom Wade
Albert Sharpe	Mr. Fletcher
Josephine Hutchinson	Mrs. Sheldon
Charles Kemper	Mr. Steuben
John Miljan	Mr. Eckert
Norma Varden	H. H. Hamilton
Carol Brannan	Bernice Eckert
Patti Brady	Sis Sheldon
Gregory Marshall	Mark Sheldon
Patsy Creighton	Sally Wilson

Screenplay by Lionel Houser
Directed by Richard Wallace
Produced by Richard H. Burger

Minister Robert Young and wife Josephine Hutchinson have a large lively family, but Shirley causes all the trouble.

MR. BELVEDERE GOES TO COLLEGE

Twentieth Century-Fox; production #753.

Mr. Belvedere needs a college degree to qualify for a special award he has won, but he will be expelled if there is any publicity. Shirley, with a son to support, works hard for publicity that pays. So they clash, then both win.

Big news was Shirley's new haircut, plus her baby in the film coinciding with the birth of her real-life baby, Linda Susan Agar, on January 30, 1948. Shirley's return to Twentieth Century-Fox earned her a big celebration with costars and staff. Comparing the film's production number (753) to *Young People* (467), made in 1940 when Shirley left the studio (unless numbers were changed), gives an idea of the studio's film output.

Clifton Webb .... Lynn Belvedere
Shirley Temple .... Ellen Baker
Tom Drake .... Bill Chase
Alan Young .... Avery Brubaker
Jessie Royce Landis .... Mrs. Chase, Tom's mother
Kathleen Hughes .... Kay Nelson
Taylor Holmes .... Dr. Gibbs
Alvin Greenman .... Corny Whittaker
Paul Harvey .... Dr. Keating
Barry Kelly .... Griggs
Bob Patten .... Joe Fisher
Lee MacGregor .... Hickey
Helen Westcott .... Marian
Jeff Chandler .... Pratt, policeman
Clancy Cooper .... McCarthy
Eevelynn Eaton .... Sally
Judy Brubaker .... Barbara
Kathleen Freeman .... Babe
Lotte Stein .... Marta
Peggy Call .... Jean Anchincloss
Ruth Tobey .... Nancy
Elaine Ryan .... Peggy
Pattee Chapman .... Isabelle
Joyce Otis .... Fluffy
Lonnie Thomas .... Davy
Reginald Sheffield .... Professor Ives
Colin Campbell .... Professor Lindley
Katherine Lang .... Miss Cadwaller
Isabel Withers .... Mrs. Myrtle
Arthur Space .... instructor
Gil Stratton, Jr. .... Beanie

Story by Gwen Davenport,
based on a character in her *Sitting Pretty*
Directed by Elliott Nugent
Produced by Samuel G. Engel

When Mr. Belvedere, Clifton Webb, registers for college, school journalist Shirley smells a story.

If Mr. Belvedere can get his degree, he will win a literary prize he badly needs. Tom Drake watches as his love interest, Shirley, tries to get a scoop, unaware that it will ruin Belvedere.

Shirley's homecoming party back at Twentieth Century-Fox includes Jane Withers with husband Bill Moss and, of course, Darryl F. Zanuck.

THE STORY OF SEABISCUIT

Warner Brothers; production #719.

This was truly the story of the great racing horse Seabiscuit—his birth, training, and competitions. Only the supporting players were different from real life. Barry Fitzgerald is the trainer; Lon McCallister is the jockey; and Shirley is Lon's love interest along with the horse. Everyone is finally victorious.

Critics panned Shirley's Irish brogue, but fans were satisfied. They worried more about hints that her marriage to John Agar was not going well.

Shirley Temple	Margaret O'Hara
Barry Fitzgerald	Shawn O'Hara
Lon McCallister	Ted Knowles
Rosemary De Camp	Mrs. Charles S. Howard
Donald MacBride	George Carson
Pierre Watkin	Charles S. Howard
William Forrest	Thomas Miltford
Sugarfoot Anderson	Murphy
Wm. J. Cartledge	Jockey George Woolf
Seabiscuit	via genuine footage

Screenplay by John Taintor Foote
Directed by David Butler

(Opposite) Lon McCallister, with Seabiscuit and Shirley, whose hair almost matches.

Nurse Shirley worries about Barry Fitzgerald's health. He worries about the horse.

A KISS FOR CORLISS

United Artists, independently produced by Enterprise Studios
at General Service; production #KC.

Boyfriend Dexter accidentally keeps Shirley/Corliss out all night. She feigns amnesia, reverting to her ten-year-old self so that her volatile father won't kill Dexter. But she has daydreamed about suave David Niven and written up an imaginary love affair in her diary. Her father finds it—then Niven is in danger.

The film was supposedly a sequel to *Kiss and Tell*, but it was different in many respects. In *Kiss*, Darryl Hickman had played Shirley's brother; now he was her boyfriend. And Shirley got new actors for both parents. The character Mildred was now single and childless.

Actor David Niven could barely stand his role in *A Kiss for Corliss*. In fact, the film was so bad that its theme of love and romance wasn't hurt by news of Shirley's filing for divorce from John Agar on December 5, 1949. The film was still a fiasco when released under a new title, *Almost a Bride*.

Shirley Temple .... Corliss Archer
David Niven .... Kenneth Marquis
Tom Tully .... Mr. Archer
Gloria Holden .... Mrs. Archer
Virginia Welles .... Mildred
Darryl Hickman .... Dexter Franklin
Robert Ellis .... Raymond Archer
Richard Craig .... Taylor

Story based on characters created by F. Hugh Herbert
Screenplay by Howard Dimsdale
Directed by Richard Wallace
Produced by Colin Miller

Shirley, pretending to be ten years old, blows bubbles at her father, Tom Tully. Her mother, Gloria Holden, tries to calm him.

INDEX